Breaking Bread Around the World

With Dedra L. Stevenson

Written, conceptualized and compiled by Dedra L. Stevenson

The following cookbook contains common foods prepared in the countries listed, and therefore, the recipes may be easily sourced from various places; however, the recipes in this book have been adapted by Ms. Dedra L. Stevenson to meet Islamic dietary requirements. Many have been adapted to become vegan versions of popular recipes, and vegetarian versions as well. All the recipes have been prepared and tested by Ms. Stevenson, and adapted to represent an easy preparation method so that readers may find the dishes simple to prepare. Any similarities to common recipes is therefore coincidental and unintentional.

Editing and Book Design by Rodney W. Harper

Assistant Editing and Book Design by Mira Al Mheiri and Shanaya Khan

Special thanks to No Prisoners No Mercy Podcast

To the people of this world, in the hope that they will all take the time to get to know each other a little better and treat each other with less aggression and more compassion.

Table of Content

Welcome to everyone everywhere, from every corner of this big blue ball that we call home! My name is Dedra L. Stevenson, and I'm an author of multi genre novels, but this time, I wanted to combine my love for cooking with my love for all things international. After all, we're one big human family, and there's no better way to make friends with people than to break bread with them. I'm so happy that you've come to join me on this culinary journey around the world.

About 3 years ago, in my home of The United Arab Emirates, I found myself about to begin another Ramadan season. Ramadan is a 30 day occasion where Muslims from around the world fast from sun up till sun down to purify their souls and learn to be more generous, give more thanks, spend more time in worship and spiritual reflection, and enjoy closeness with family. The Iftar meal, or breakfast, is eaten at night, after the evening call to prayer.

I really wanted to make Ramadan more fun for my family, so I decided to prepare an Iftar from a different nation's cuisine each day. By doing this, I figured that I'd be teaching my children about international culture, teaching tolerance, and making Ramadan a lot more festive and fun in my own home.

Well, the idea was a hit! I started posting on Social Media, and everyone started to tune in daily to see what country I'd be visiting today!

So, let's get ready to hop on my magic carpet and visit 30 countries in this first volume of the series. The recipes are easy to prepare, and have all been tested and adjusted by me. I hope you get just as much excitement out of doing this as I did!

Have a wonderful journey!

Your friend,
Dedra L. Stevenson, www.bluejinnimedia.com

AFGHANISTAN

Dedra's Notes

Afghani cuisine is well known in the United Arab Emirates and all through the region.

It's a favorite in many homes, as the food is often regarded as sweet and savory at the same time. I must admit that I really had my reservations about trying this cuisine, but it proved to be one of the tastiest, and since alphabetically, it's first in my line up, you can try it right away and see for yourself.

This one has a vegan main course option.

Menu

Starter

Mantu

Entree

Qabuli Pulao

– or –

Qorma-e-Lubia

Dessert

Baklava

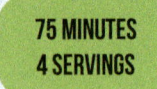
Starter

When I made this, I did it without the topping, and only used the dip. I fried the dumplings instead of putting them into the oven. It was wonderful, so feel free to ditch the topping if you don't have time. It works without it also.

Mantu

FILLING INGREDIENTS	FOR THE TOPPING	FOR THE YOGURT DIP
1 3/4 CUPS OF ONION 1 POUND OF GROUND BEEF/LAMB ½ TSP. GARLIC 2 TSP. CORIANDER POWDER ½ TSP. SALT ½ TSP. BLACK PEPPER POWDER	1 CUP BROWN LENTILS ½ POUND GROUND BEEF/LAMB 1 MEDIUM ONION (FINELY CHOPPED) ½ TSP. GARLIC ½ TSP. SALT ½ TSP. BLACK PEPPER POWDER 2 TSP. TOMATO PASTE 40 ML. COOKING OIL	1 TSP. DRIED MINT LEAVES ½ TSP. GARLIC ½ TSP. SALT 500 ML PLAIN YOGURT

Method for Filling

Heat pan over a medium heat and add garlic, ground beef and salt and coriander. Cook until the meat is half-way cooked for about 15 to 20 minutes. Add black pepper and remove from heat.
Combine one cup of raw chopped onions to the meat and let it cool down to room temperature

Method for Sauce Topping

Soak split peas for 2–3 hours or overnight.
Heat oil in a frying pan and cook onion and garlic until lightly browned.
Add tomato and tomato paste. Add split peas and ¾ cup water and cook for 30–45 minutes until soft.
Season with salt and pepper and set aside.

Method for Yogurt Dip

Combine all of the ingredients for dip in a bowl and mix well.
Method for Pastry (if making, but I suggest you buy a store bought variety to save time. I did.)
Place flour in a large mixing bowl and gradually add water, mixing with hands until it becomes doughy.
Leave the dough to settle for 15–20 minutes or until firm.
Separate dough into small handfuls and roll into individual ball shapes.
Scatter some flour on the bench surface and using a small rolling pin, roll the balls into circular shapes.

Making the Mantu

Roll the dough ball into a very thin strips. Cut the strips into 2-inch squares.
Place approximately one tablespoon of the cooled ground beef and onion mixture onto each wrap. To make the wraps stick together easily, wet the edges with water (you may use your fingers or a basting brush).

Entree

Qabuli Pulao

MEAT INGREDIENTS

1KG LAMB LEG OR SHOULDER, ON THE BONE,
CHOPPED INTO 6 CM PIECE
1 ONION, CHOPPED
3 GARLIC
1 CUP WATER

CARROT & RAISINS MIX INGREDIENTS

4 CARROTS, PEELED
1 CUP RAISINS
6 TBSP VEGETABLE OIL
1 TBSP SUGAR

RICE INGREDIENTS

1 KG SELLA BASMATI RICE, SOAKED IN COLD
WATER FOR 4 HOURS OR OVERNIGHT
10 CUP WATER
3 TBSP SALT
½ CUP OIL
4 TBSP SUGAR
1 TSP CUMIN
1 CUP MEAT BROTH

Qabuli pulao is the most popular dish in Afghanistan, and is considered the national dish. It is a made by cooking basmati or long grained rice in a brothy sauce (which makes the rice brown). This dish may be made with lamb, chicken, or beef. Qabili Palau is baked in the oven and topped with fried sliced carrots and raisins. Chopped nuts like pistachios or almonds may be added as well. The meat is covered by the rice or buried in the middle of the dish.

Soak rice in water in a bowl and keep aside.

Heat oil in a pressure cooker and fry onions with garlic until golden brown. Add meat pieces to the fried onion and cook until light brown on both sides. Add water (boiled) and bring to a boil. Lower the heat and simmer covered until meat is tender. Add more water if required.

In a separate pan, sauté carrots, in a small quantity of oil, add sugar and ¼ cup water and and fry until softened. Remove from pan and keep aside. Add a little oil to the pan and sauté raisins until they swell up. Add carrots and mix it with raisin. Remove from pan and set aside.

Place 4 tbsp sugar in a hot, dry saucepan over medium heat. Cook, shaking pan, for 5–6 minutes or until sugar has caramelized. Carefully add ½ cup oil, 1 tbsp salt, meat broth and cumin. Bring to the boil, then remove from heat and set aside.

Drain the soaked rice. Cook in a large saucepan of boiling water with 2 tbsp salt for 10 minutes, or until almost cooked. Drain and return to pan. Pour over the caramelized sugar mixture and stir until rice is evenly coated. Mix rise will and sing the end of a large spoon, make holes all over rice to allow it to steam evenly.

Top with spiced carrot and reserved lamb. Cover and seal pan with a tea towel, then a lid. Place over low heat and cook for 5 minutes, or until you hear a ticking sound. Reduce the heat to low and cook for another 30 minutes. Remove from the heat.

Remove lamb and spiced carrots, and mix rice well. To serve, cover base of a platter with a little rice, spoon over the lamb and then cover with remaining rice. Top with spiced carrot.

Entree

Qorma-e-Lubia

INGREDIENTS

1 CAN OF RED KIDNEY BEANS
½ ONION (FINELY CHOPPED)
3 TABLESPOONS OIL
2 TABLESPOONS CORIANDER
1 TEASPOON TURMERIC
3 CLOVES GARLIC (MINCED)
1 TEASPOON GROUND CUMIN
2 TABLESPOONS TOMATO SAUCE
CRUSHED DRIED MINT (OPTIONAL)
2 CUPS WATER
GROUND RED CHILI PEPPER TO TASTE
SALT

Drain and rinse the kidney beans and set aside.

Heat the oil on medium high heat and caramelize the onions until light golden brown.

Add the beans, water, coriander, salt, pepper, turmeric, garlic, cumin, and tomato sauce. Stir.

Cover the pot and cook on medium heat for about 15-20 minutes. Cook until the water has reduced and the oil has surfaced to the top.

Once it is ready, mix in crushed dried mint (optional).

Serve with Chalau.

Dessert

Baklava

INGREDIENTS

FILLO DOUGH (RECIPE BELOW, BUT STORE BOUGHT WILL ALSO DO)
1/2-POUND BUTTER (UNSALTED)
1 TSP. CINNAMON POWDER
1 1/4 CUPS SUGAR
1 TSP. CARDAMOM
ALMONDS (FINE SLICED)
1 TSP. FRESH LEMON JUICE
1 1/2 CUPS WATER
CRUSHED PISTACHIOS

First, preheat the oven to 375 degrees. Next, melt the butter over very low heat. Combine freshly ground cardamom cinnamon in a small bowl. Lay two layers of Fillo dough on a baking sheet, and pour two tablespoons of melted butter over the dough. Use a pastry brush to spread the butter.

Next, sprinkle a thin layer of fresh almond nuts, and a small amount of the cinnamon/cardamom mixture. Repeat this until you have several layers. On the top layer, only spread melted butter. Bake the baklava at 375 degrees, until the Fillo dough is golden brown. At this point, remove the baklava from the oven and prepare the syrup.

For the syrup… Combine one and one-half cups of water with one and a quarter cups of sugar, and one teaspoon of fresh lemon juice. Bring the mix to a boil, turn down the heat and simmer for 5 minutes. While the baklava is still warm, cut it into small triangle shapes and drizzle the syrup over the baklava. To finish, sprinkle with crushed pistachio nuts. (If you're not a fan of pistachios, you can skip this step)

FILLO DOUGH INGREDIENTS

3 ½ TO 4 ½ CUPS FINELY GROUND DURUM SEMOLINA
1 SCANT TEASPOON SALT
1 ¼ CUPS WATER
½ CUP EXTRA-VIRGIN OLIVE OIL, PLUS MORE FOR THE BOWL
1 TABLESPOON RED-WINE VINEGAR OR LEMON JUICE
SALT

Prepare the Fillo Dough

In the bowl of a mixer fitted with a dough hook, combine 3 1/4 cups of the flour and salt. Add the water, olive oil and vinegar or lemon juice. Mix on low speed for 3 minutes, then increase speed to medium. Knead with the hook, stopping the mixer to add additional flour in 1/4-cup increments as needed, until the dough is very smooth and pliant. The whole mixing process should take about 10 to 12 minutes.

Transfer the dough to an oiled bowl. Cover tightly with plastic wrap, and let stand for 1 hour at room temperature. You can store the dough, well wrapped, in the refrigerator for several days or in the freezer for up to two weeks. Bring to room temperature before using. (If it's frozen, first defrost in the refrigerator.)

Australia

Dedra's Notes

Australia was one of my favorite countries because I have been there for one of the best vacations of my life! The country is crazy gorgeous, and the people are some of the friendliest in the entire world! I enjoyed learning about Aboriginal culture, the wonderful work in the preservation of wildlife, and the love for all things natural and wholesome. I think that the cuisine is definitely a reflection of the sunny disposition that most Australians share. If you ever get the chance to go, just say YES!

Menu

Starter

Potato Dumplings

Entree

Australian Tuna Bake

– or –

Mince and Potato Hot Pot

Dessert

Australian Style Pumpkin Scones

Starter

Potato Dumplings

INGREDIENTS

2 POUNDS OF POTATO

ALL PURPOSE FLOUR AS NEEDED

½ TEASPOON NUTMEG

3 EGGS BEATEN

2 OUNCES SALTED BUTTER MELTED AND COOLED

Boil the potatoes until tender.

Set aside until completely cold.

Grate cold potatoes into a large bowl.

Add half the grated potato in flour and mix well together.

Add the nutmeg, the melted butter and the beaten egg.

Form into small dumpling shapes with slightly damp hands.

Bring a large pot of water to boil.

Place a few dumplings into the fast boiling water, and cook for about 10 minutes.

Lift from water with a slotted spoon and drain.

Cook remainder of dumplings a few at a time, until completed.

Ok, this step is optional, but if you want to change this a bit, you can Deep fry the dumplings. (Maybe it's my Southern background talking here?)

Sauce is great with this dish, so go ahead and serve with the recommended sauce of tomato and onion, flavored with a little thyme and oregano, or a sauce of your choice.

Entree

Australian Tuna Bake

INGREDIENTS

1/2 CUP CHEESE, SHREDDED
1 CUP CRUSHED CORN FLAKES
12 OUNCES CANNED TUNA
4 TABLESPOONS BUTTER, PLUS A LITTLE MORE FOR THE TOP OF THE CASSEROLE
4 TABLESPOONS FLOUR
2 CUPS MILK
1 ONION, FINELY CHOPPED
1 CUP PEAS (COOKED OR FROZEN)
SALT AND PEPPER
1 TOMATO, CUT INTO 8 WEDGES
½ CUP FRESH PARSLEY, CHOPPED
1 LEMON CUT INTO 4 WEDGES
1 CUP COOKED PASTA SPIRAL

MY FAMILY ARE SPLIT BETWEEN FISH LOVERS AND THOSE WHO DON'T CARE FOR FISH DISHES, BUT THIS ONE WAS A BIG HIT WITH THE FISH LOVERS. IT ALSO FREEZES BEAUTIFULLY IN CASE YOU CAN'T FINISH IT ALL!

Preheat oven to 350°F and grease an 8x8-inch casserole dish.

Melt the butter in a sauté pan. Sauté the onion until soft but not browned. Add the flour and blend with the onion. Add the milk, stirring constantly. Bring to the boil and boil for 2 or 3 minutes. Remove from heat.

Stir in the shredded cheese, cooked pasta, peas, tuna and seasonings. Pour into the casserole. Cover with crushed corn flakes, dot with butter, and bake for 20-30 minutes.

Sprinkle parsley over the top of the hot casserole. Garnish with tomato wedges and lemon wedges. Serve hot. It's great with a tossed salad on the side.

Entree

Shearers' Mince and Potato Hot Pot

This is a great outback recipe often prepared for the sheep shearers. Delicious!! Try serving it with some steamed mixed veggies of your choice.

INGREDIENTS

1 TABLESPOON OLIVE OIL

1-POUND GROUND BEEF

1 ONION, CHOPPED

1 TABLESPOON PARSLEY

1 1/2 TABLESPOON TOMATO SAUCE

1 TABLESPOON WORCESTERSHIRE SAUCE

SALT AND PEPPER TO TASTE

¼ CUP BUTTER

2 CUPS MILK

1 CUP SHREDDED SHARP CHEDDAR CHEESE

1 (6 OUNCE) CAN MUSHROOMS, DRAINED (OPTIONAL IF YOU DON'T LIKE MUSHROOMS)

2 TABLESPOONS BUTTER, DICED

Preheat oven to 350 degrees F (175 degrees C). Place potato slices in a medium bowl with enough water to cover.

Heat oil in a medium saucepan over medium heat. Stir in ground beef, and cook until evenly browned, drain excess fat and next add the onion, tomato sauce, and Worcestershire sauce. Season with salt and pepper. Cook until onions are tender.

In a separate medium saucepan over medium heat, melt 1/4 cup butter, and thoroughly blend in flour. Gradually stir in milk. Cook and stir 5 minutes, or until thickened. Reduce heat, and blend Cheddar cheese into the mixture. Season with salt and pepper to taste.

Line a medium baking dish with 1/2 the potato slices. Pour in the ground beef mixture, and top with mushrooms. Cover with the cheese sauce mixture. Top with remaining potatoes. Dot with 2 tablespoons butter.

Bake 40 minutes in the preheated oven, until lightly browned.

Dessert

Australian-Style Pumpkin Scones

INGREDIENTS

1 TABLESPOON BUTTER, AT ROOM TEMPERATURE

2 CUPS SELF-RISING FLOUR

½ CUP WHITE SUGAR

1 TEASPOON BAKING POWDER

¼ TEASPOON SALT

1 CUP COOKED AND MASHED PUMPKIN

1 EGG

PLEASE NOTE THAT THESE ARE GREAT FOR AN AFTER DINNER COFFEE (OR TEA), BUT THEY ARE ALSO ABSOLUTELY AMAZING FOR BREAKFAST!

Preheat oven to 450 degrees F (230 degrees C).

Rub butter into flour in a bowl using your fingers until evenly combined. Add sugar, baking powder, and salt to flour mixture; make a well in the center.

Mix pumpkin and egg together in a separate bowl; pour into the well and mix until dough is well combined.

Turn dough onto a floured work surface and cut into squares using a knife with flour on it.

Arrange squares or circles on a baking sheet.

Bake in the preheated oven until lightly browned, 15 to 20 minutes.

BOLIVIA

THE LAND OF CONTRASTS

From the majestic peaks of the Andes Mountains to the Rainforests, Bolivia is a land of contrasts. Its natural beauty is stunning, and the people are amazingly hospitable, as I'm told. I haven't had the pleasure of visiting this country, but someone close to me has, and I was inspired to try some of the food. My family loved it, and I remember that

they commented on how similar it tastes to Spanish cuisine. If you visit Bolivia, I'm told that your food budget needn't be very high, and for such low costs, you get a generous portion. Sadly, I've only prepared one main dish from this country, but I'm sure that you'll love it.

Menu

Starter

Saltenas

Entree

Picante de Pollo

– or –

Papitas

Dessert

Cocadas

Starter

Saltenas

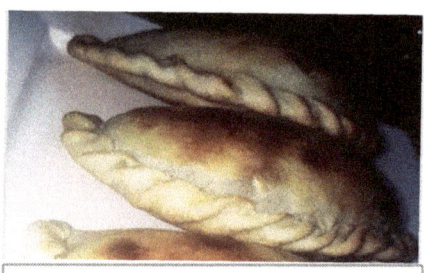

Sprinkle the gelatin over the 1/2 cup cold water in a heatproof dish; set aside for 10 minutes. Microwave the rehydrated gelatin for 30 seconds or until melted (or melt it over a pot of simmering water). Transfer the melted gelatin to a small bowl and refrigerate until set.

Place the potatoes into a medium saucepan, cover with water, and bring to a boil over medium heat. Reduce heat, and simmer until the potatoes are cooked but still firm, about 10 minutes. Remove from water, allow to cool, and shred into a bowl, then set aside.

Heat the olive oil in a skillet over medium heat. Stir in the onion, and then cook and stir until the onion has softened and turned translucent, about 5 minutes.

Add the ground beef, and cook until the meat is no longer pink, breaking it up into crumbles as it cooks, about 10 minutes. Drain excess grease.

Stir in the shredded potatoes, peas, spring onion, parsley, 4 tsp. sugar, 2 teaspoons paprika, cumin, salt and black pepper, and 3 tablespoons jalapeno sauce (optional). Simmer filling until hot, about 3 minutes. Remove from heat and set aside.

Preheat an oven to 425 degrees F (220 degrees C). Lightly grease a baking sheet, or line it with parchment paper.

Combine the flour, 1/4 cup sugar, and 1 teaspoon of salt. Cut in the butter with a knife or pastry blender until the mixture resembles coarse crumbs. (This can also be done in a food processor: pulse the butter and flour mixture until it looks like cornmeal. Turn mixture into a bowl and proceed.) Slowly add the hot water and knead until smooth, about 3 minutes.

Keep the dough covered with plastic wrap or a clean kitchen towel to keep it warm. Divide the dough into 16 pieces and roll them into balls. Keep the other balls of dough covered with a towel while you roll out each round.

On a lightly floured surface, roll each ball of dough into a 1/8-inch-thick circle. Whisk the beaten eggs and 2 teaspoons water in a small bowl. Lightly brush egg wash on the edges of the dough circle. Place about 2 tablespoons of the meat filling on one half of the dough round; top it with about a 1/2 teaspoon of hard-boiled egg, 1/4 teaspoon of gelatin, a few sliced black olives, and some raisins.

Fold the dough over the filling. Seal and scallop the edges of the dough together. To scallop, start at one edge of the half circle: fold a small piece of dough (the size of your fingernail) over the seam and press gently. Fold another small piece of dough over the seam so that it overlaps the first piece; repeat until you have sealed the half circle. (You may also seal the Saltenas by pressing a fork around edges.)

Place the saltena on the prepared baking sheet and continue with the remaining dough and filling. Whisk the paprika into the remaining egg wash and brush the Saltenas with the egg wash. Bake in the preheated oven until golden brown, 15 to 20 minutes.

INGREDIENTS (FILLING)

1 (.25 OUNCE) PACKAGE UNFLAVORED GELATIN
3 POTATOES, PEELED
1 1/2 TABLESPOONS OLIVE OIL
1 ONION, CHOPPED
1 1/2 POUNDS GROUND BEEF
1 (10 OUNCE) PACKAGE FROZEN PETITE PEAS, THAWED
1 SPRING ONION, SLICED
1/2 CUP FRESH PARSLEY, CHOPPED
4 TEASPOONS WHITE SUGAR
2 ½ TEASPOONS PAPRIKA
1/2 TEASPOON GROUND CUMIN
1 1/2 TEASPOONS SALT
1/4 TEASPOON BLACK PEPPER
3 TABLESPOONS JALAPENO SAUCE (OPTIONAL)
1/2 CUP COLD WATER
3 HARD-COOKED EGGS, PEELED AND CHOPPED
1 (2.25 OUNCE) CAN SLICED BLACK OLIVES, DRAINED
1 CUP RAISINS, SOAKED IN WATER AND DRAINED

DOUGH INGREDIENTS

6 CUPS ALL-PURPOSE FLOUR
1/4 CUP WHITE SUGAR
1 TEASPOON SALT
1 CUP BUTTER, CUBED
1 1/2 CUPS HOT WATER
2 EGGS, BEATEN
2 TEASPOONS WATER
1 TABLESPOON PAPRIKA

Entree

Picante de Pollo

INGREDIENTS

1 ½ KG. CHICKEN, DIVIDED INTO PARTS

¼ CUP GROUND CAYENNE PEPPER

2 CUPS OF WHITE ONION, CUT INTO SMALL STRIPS

1 CUP TOMATO, PEELED AND FINELY CHOPPED

½ CUP FRESH CHILI PEPPER, FINELY CHOPPED

1 CUP GREEN PEAS, PEELED

½ CUP PARSLEY, FINELY CHOPPED

1 TEASPOON GROUND CUMIN

1 TEASPOON CRUMBLED OREGANO

½ TEASPOON GROUND BLACK PEPPER

1 TABLESPOON SALT

3 GARLIC CLOVES, PEELED, CHOPPED AND ROASTED

3 CUPS BROTH OR WATER

2 SPOONFUL OIL

In a large casserole put the chicken pieces with all the other ingredients. Pour the broth or water until covering the ingredients completely.

Set to cook over high heat until it boils, and later over low heat for at least an hour and a half or until the chicken is soft.

Stir occasionally. If while cooking the broth diminished much, add a little bit more of broth or water so that when serving there is enough liquid.

In a deep plate serve one piece of spicy chicken with rice, one boiled potato, both cooked aside and uncooked tomato and onion salad on top. Finally, sprinkle the chopped parsley on top of the spicy chicken.

Entree

Papitas

INGREDIENTS

1 LB. QUINOA

5 EGGS

5 SLICES WHITE BREAD

½ CUP MILK (TO SOAK THE BREAD)

16 OZ. CANNED TUNA IN WATER, WELL DRAINED

2 LEMONS

1 CHILI PEPPER, FINELY CHOPPED

VEGETABLE OIL (FOR FRYING)

SALT

PEPPER

Rinse the quinoa in a very fine strainer until the water is clear.

Cook for 15 minutes in 2 times its volume of water (about 6 cups), covered and do not salt until the end of cooking. Drain and let cool in a colander.

In a salad bowl, mix the cooked quinoa with 2 whole eggs and the bread slices soaked in milk until obtaining a smooth paste.

In another bowl, make the stuffing by mixing the tuna, the remaining 3 eggs, the lemon zest and juice, the chili pepper, salt and pepper.

Take a ball of quinoa in the palm of your hand, make a hole in it with your thumb and put some tuna stuffing.

Add a little quinoa preparation to close the patty, then press on the whole thing to form the shape of a ball, which will be flattened a little before frying.

Fry the papitas in a large bath of hot oil (at about 350 F).

Wait at least 2 minutes before turning them over. The bottom must form a crust and reach a golden brown color to prevent the papitas from breaking when flipping.

When they are golden brown on both sides, place them on a plate lined with paper towels

Dessert

Cocadas

INGREDIENTS

3 1/2 CUPS SHREDDED SWEETENED COCONUT

3/4 CUP SWEETENED CONDENSED MILK

2 1/2 TABLESPOONS CORNSTARCH

1/2 TEASPOON ALMOND EXTRACT

1 TEASPOON VANILLA EXTRACT

½ CUP CONFECTIONERS' SUGAR (OPTIONAL)

Preheat oven to 400 degrees F.

In a medium mixing bowl, stir together coconut, cornstarch, condensed milk, almond extract, and vanilla extract. Let mixture sit for 3 to 5 minutes.

Using 2 tablespoons, drop by heaping rounded spoonfuls onto parchment lined cookie sheet about 1-inch apart.

Watching closely, bake for 15 to 20 minutes until lightly golden brown. Remove from oven and cool on wire rack.

Using fine mesh sifter, dust with confectioners' sugar. Store loosely covered until ready to serve. This is easy and really delicious!

CANADA

Dedra's Notes

Canada is one of the most beautiful countries in the world in terms of natural beauty. Its weather is challenging, but Canadians are strong and capable, prepared for any contingency. Sadly, I've never had the pleasure of visiting, but I'd like to one day. That's the great thing about food. Even if you can't be there physically, you can visit any culture via your kitchen, so why not invite others to enjoy the Canadian cuisine?

Menu

Starter

Mini Pizza Bites

Entree

Tourtiere

– or –

Maple Glazed Salmon

Dessert

Beaver Tails

Starter

Mini Pizza Bites

INGREDIENTS

1 (8 OUNCE) CANS REFRIGERATED DINNER ROLLS

1 (8 OUNCE) JARS PIZZA SAUCE

4 SLICES MOZZARELLA CHEESE

16 PEPPERONIS (I PREFER BEEF), OR MINI TOMATO
SLICES IF YOU WANT THIS TO BE VEGETARIAN

A FEW OLIVES (OPTIONAL)

Preheat oven to 375.

Place rolls on ungreased baking sheet try to flatten rolls so they resemble flat circles.

Take a spoonful of sauce and spread each roll.

Grate cheese into small bits and garnish.

Place the slices (either pepperoni or small tomato slices) on top of the cheese and cover the slices with the remaining shredded cheese.

Place a few olives in the cheese. Black olives are best with pizza.

Cook for about 15 min of until rolls are golden.

Entree

French Canadian Tourtiere

INGREDIENTS

1 ½ POUND LEAN GROUND BEEF

1 ONION, DICED

1 CLOVE GARLIC, MINCED

½ CUP WATER

1 ½ TEASPOONS SALT

½ TEASPOON DRIED THYME, CRUSHED

¼ TEASPOON GROUND SAGE

¼ TEASPOON GROUND BLACK PEPPER

1/8 TEASPOON GROUND CLOVES

1 RECIPE PASTRY FOR A 9-INCH DOUBLE CRUST PIE

PLEASE NOTE THAT THIS RECIPE IS MY OWN TAKE ON THIS DISH, AS IN ALL DISHES IN THIS BOOK, BUT THIS IS ONE OF THE DISHES THAT JUST HAPPENED TO NORMALLY CONTAIN PORK. NORMALLY, THE DISH IS HALF GROUND BEEF AND HALF PORK, BUT I CAN TELL YOU THAT IT TASTES AMAZING WITH JUST THE BEEF.

In a saucepan, combine beef, onion, garlic, water, salt, thyme, sage, black pepper and cloves. Cook over medium heat until mixture boils; stirring occasionally. Reduce heat to low and simmer until meat is cooked, about 5 minutes. Allow to cool to room temperature.

Preheat oven to 425 degrees F (220 degrees C).

Spoon the meat mixture into the pie crust. Place top crust on top of pie and pinch edges to seal. Cut slits in top crust so steam can escape. Cover edges of pie with strips of aluminum foil. (So the edges don't get burned)

Bake in preheated oven for 20 minutes; remove foil and return to oven. Bake for an additional 15 to 20 minutes, or until golden brown. Let cool 10 minutes before slicing.

Entree

Maple Salmon

INGREDIENTS

1/4 CUP MAPLE SYRUP

2 TABLESPOONS SOY SAUCE

1 CLOVE GARLIC, MINCED

¼ TEASPOON GARLIC SALT

1 TSP. PARSLEY

1/8 TEASPOON GROUND BLACK PEPPER

1-POUND SALMON

In a small bowl, mix the maple syrup, soy sauce, garlic, garlic salt, and pepper.

Place salmon in a shallow glass baking dish, and coat with the maple syrup mixture. Cover the dish, and marinate salmon in the refrigerator 30 to 45 minutes, turning once.

Preheat oven to 400 degrees F (200 degrees C).

Place the baking dish in the preheated oven, and bake salmon uncovered 20 minutes, or until easily flaked with a fork.

Garnish with Parsley.

Dessert

Beaver Tails

INGREDIENTS

1/2 CUP VERY WARM WATER

5 TEASPOONS DRY YEAST

SUGAR, JUST A PINCH OR TWO

1 CUP WARM MILK

1/3 CUP SUGAR

1 1/2 TEASPOONS SALT

1 TEASPOON VANILLA

2 EGGS

1/3 CUP OIL

4 1/4 - 5 CUPS UNBLEACHED ALL-PURPOSE FLOUR

OIL (FOR FRYING)

GRANULATED SUGAR (FOR DUSTING)

CINNAMON

In a large mixing bowl, stir together the yeast, warm water and pinch (or two) of sugar.

Allow to stand a couple of minutes to allow yeast to swell or dissolve.

Stir in remaining sugar, milk, vanilla, eggs, oil, salt, and most of flour to make soft dough.

Knead 5-8 minutes (by hand or with a dough hook), adding flour as needed to form a firm, smooth, elastic dough.

Place in a greased bowl. Place bowl in a plastic bag and seal. (If not using right away, you can refrigerate the dough at this point).

Let rise in a covered, lightly greased bowl; about 30-40 minutes.

Gently deflate dough. (If dough is coming out of the fridge, allow to warm up for about 40 minutes before proceeding).

Pinch off a golf ball-sized piece of dough. Roll out into an oval and let rest, covered with a tea towel, while you are preparing the remaining dough.

Heat about 4 inches of oil in fryer (a wok works best, but you can use a Dutch oven or whatever you usually use for frying). Temperature of the oil should be about 385°F.

Add the dough pieces to the hot oil, about 1-2 at a time.

BUT -- before you do, stretch the ovals into a tail shape, like a beaver's tail - thinning them out and enlarging them as you do. (You can have a lot of fun with this, making the tails in any shape you want really)

Turn once to fry until all sides are deep brown.

Lift the tails out with tongs and drain on paper towels.

Fill a large bowl with a few cups of white sugar.

Toss the tails in sugar (with a little cinnamon if you wish) and shake off excess.

Try whatever topping you like on these—jam, pie filling, etc. Yummy!

CHINA

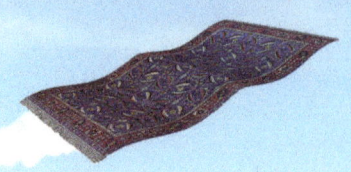

Dedra's Notes

Visiting China was one of the most exciting and adventurous moments of my entire life. Seeing the Forbidden City and the Great Wall made me feel that I was walking through the pages of the ancient past. I loved every moment, and the people were very kind and helpful. Shopping in the Silk Market was a great time, and gave us the chance to use our bargaining power, and nothing makes you feel like sitting down to a great Chinese meal like shopping! Enjoy your Chinese menu, and try to eat it with chopsticks if you can. It makes the experience so much better.

Menu

Starter

Green Onion Cakes (Vegan)

Entree

Shrimp with Broccoli in Garlic Sauce

– or –

Chinese Garlic Chicken

Dessert

Chinese Almond Cookies

Starter

Green Onion Cakes

INGREDIENTS

3 CUPS BREAD FLOUR

1 ¼ CUPS BOILING WATER

2 TABLESPOONS VEGETABLE OIL

SALT AND PEPPER TO TASTE

1 BUNCH GREEN ONIONS, FINELY CHOPPED

1 TEASPOONS VEGETABLE OIL, OR AS NEEDED

Use a fork to mix flour and boiling water in a large bowl. Knead dough into a ball. Cover bowl with plastic wrap; let dough rest for 30 to 60 minutes.

Evenly divide dough into 16 pieces. Roll each piece into a 1/4-inch-thick circle. Brush each circle with oil, season with salt and pepper, and sprinkle with about 1 teaspoon of green onions. Roll up, cigar style; coil each pancake and pinch open ends together to form a disc. Roll each circle flat to about 1/4-inch thickness.

Heat 2 teaspoons oil in a large skillet. Fry cakes until golden brown, about 2 minutes on each side. Add more oil between batches, if necessary.

Entree

Shrimp with Broccoli in Garlic Sauce

INGREDIENTS

1 TABLESPOON WATER

2 TABLESPOONS PEANUT OIL

4 LARGE CLOVES GARLIC, MINCED

1 CUP LOW-SODIUM CHICKEN BROTH (I USED AN ORGANIC VEGETABLE BROTH)

1 TABLESPOON SOY SAUCE

1 TABLESPOON OYSTER SAUCE

2 TEASPOONS GRATED FRESH GINGER ROOT

1-POUND UNCOOKED MEDIUM SHRIMP, PEELED AND DEVEINED

¼ CUP CANNED WATER CHESTNUTS, DRAINED (THIS IS OPTIONAL. I DIDN'T INCLUDE THIS AND IT TURNED OUT GREAT!)

2 TABLESPOONS CORNSTARCH

Combine broccoli and water in a glass bowl; steam in microwave oven until slightly tender, 2 to 3 minutes.

Heat peanut oil in a large skillet or wok over medium-high heat. Cook garlic in hot oil until it smells lovely, about 1 minute. Reduce heat to low; add chicken broth, soy sauce, oyster sauce, and ginger root to the garlic.

Bring the mixture to a boil and add the shrimp; cook and stir until the shrimp turn pink, 3 to 4 minutes. Toss steamed broccoli and water chestnuts with the shrimp mixture to coat with the sauce. Stir cornstarch into the mixture 1 tablespoon at a time until the sauce thickens, about 5 minutes.

Entree

45 MINUTES
4 SERVINGS

Chinese Garlic Chicken

INGREDIENTS

1 1/2 POUNDS SKINLESS, BONELESS CHICKEN BREASTS, CUT INTO BITE-SIZE PIECES

1 TEASPOON SALT

½ TEASPOON SALT

2 TABLESPOONS ALL-PURPOSE FLOUR

2 TABLESPOONS PEANUT OIL

15 CLOVES GARLIC PEELED

2 TABLESPOONS LIGHT SOY SAUCE

1 1/3 CUPS CHICKEN STOCK (I USED AN ORGANIC VEGETABLE STOCK)

SESAME SEEDS

Season chicken with salt and black pepper. Toss with flour until coated.

Heat peanut oil in a wok or large skillet over high heat until it begins to smoke. Add chicken, and stir fry until the pieces are lightly browned on the outside, 3 to 5 minutes. Turn heat to medium and stir in whole garlic cloves; continue stir frying for 5 minutes.

Turn heat to low, and soy sauce and chicken stock. Cover, and simmer for 20 minutes until the chicken is tender. Remove garlic cloves before serving.

Dessert

Chinese Almond Cookies

INGREDIENTS

1 1/3 CUPS OF ALMOND FLOUR, LIGHTLY PACKED
1 CUP OF UNSALTED BUTTER, CHILLED AND CUT INTO CUBES
PINCH OF SEA SALT
2 EGGS
1 1/2 TEASPOON OF ALMOND EXTRACT
1 3/4 CUPS OF FLOUR
1 CUP + 3 TABLESPOONS OF SUGAR
1/2 TEASPOON OF BAKING SODA
HALF CUP OF THINLY SLICED ALMONDS

Place the almond flour, salt, and butter into an electric beater and beat on medium speed for three minutes. The mixture will become coarse and chunky looking.

Add one of the eggs, reserving the other for later, and the almond extract. Mix on low speed until just incorporated.

Sift together the flour, sugar, and baking soda then add to the butter mixture at low speed. Mix until just combined.

Take the dough and flatten it into a disc and wrap in plastic wrap. Place it in the refrigerator for two hours to chill.

Preheat the oven to 325 F. Line a baking sheet with parchment paper. Place the other egg into a bowl and beat it.

Take bits of dough and roll them into balls about an inch wide. Place them on the sheet about an inch apart and then press them down slightly with your palm to make a coin shape.

Place a slivered almond onto each cookie and lightly press it into place, (or you can make a pattern) then paint the surface of the cookie with some of the beaten egg using a pastry brush or your finger (this makes the cookies a little shiny).

Bake for 13-15 minutes or until the edges just begin to brown. Cool on the sheet on a wire rack.

DENMARK

Dedra's Notes

We went to visit Denmark around the end of December, and lucky for us, we were there to see the New Year's Eve fireworks at Tivoli Gardens. Everyone was friendly, and we had no problems finding what we needed. Since we spent a lot of time out, we ate Danish style fast food, and it was delicious! Since we were looking for Halal meat, I thought we were going to have issues, but thankfully, we found several very nice restaurants. I hope that I've expressed my delight adequately with these simple recipes.

Menu

Starter

Danish Potato Salad

Entree

Danish Meatballs (Frikadeller)

– or –

Danish Burgers with Herb Caper Sauce
and a Mod Salad

Dessert

Danish Oatmeal Cookies

Starter

Danish Potato Salad

INGREDIENTS

3-POUND GOLD POTATOES

1/2 CUP CHOPPED GREEN ONIONS

1/4 CUP CHOPPED FRESH PARSLEY

½ RED ONION, THINLY SLICED

2 TABLESPOONS CAPERS, DRAINED

3 TABLESPOONS WHITE VINEGAR

1 1/2 TABLESPOONS CAPER LIQUID

1 1/2 TABLESPOONS DIJON MUSTARD

1/2 CUP + 2 TABLESPOONS OLIVE OIL

SALT AND PEPPER TO TASTE

Cook potatoes in a large pot of boiling salted water until tender, about 15 minutes.

Drain potatoes; cool 30 minutes. Peel potatoes in large bowl. Add chives, onion, parsley and capers.

Combine vinegar, caper liquid and mustard in small bowl. Whisk in oil.

Season dressing to taste with salt and pepper. (can be made several hours ahead)

Let stand at room temperature.

Entree

Danish Meatballs (Frikadeller)

INGREDIENTS

(2 CUPS) LOW-SALT HOMEMADE OR GOOD QUALITY
CHICKEN STOCK
1 KG LAMB MINCE
20 G SALT
1 BROWN ONION, FINELY CHOPPED
50G (1/3 CUP) PLAIN FLOUR
100 G DRIED BREADCRUMBS
FRESHLY GROUND BLACK PEPPER
3 EGGS
1 ½ CUPS MILK
OLIVE OIL AND BUTTER FOR PAN FRYING

Place the stock in a saucepan over medium heat and simmer for 15 minutes, or until reduced to about 125 ml.

Place the mince in a large bowl. Add the salt and combine well. Add the onion, flour and breadcrumbs, and season with black pepper.

Combine very well, then add the eggs, but of course, make sure your hands are clean before you begin. Add the reduced chicken stock mixture, then gradually add the milk and knead until well combined.

Cover and refrigerate for at least 1 hour.

To cook, heat 1 tbsp. of oil and plenty of butter in a large frying pan over medium heat. When foamy, use a dessertspoon to shape mixture into quenelles.

Cook, spooning over butter, for 6-8 minutes, or until golden on all sides and cooked through.

Serve with pickled cucumber salad or the potato salad used in this book. Chill for one hour.

Entree

Danish Burgers with Herb Caper Sauce

INGREDIENTS

2 POUNDS GROUND CHICKEN

1 TABLESPOON OF ANY GOOD POULTRY SEASONING

2 SHALLOTS, FINELY CHOPPED

2 TABLESPOONS, DIJON MUSTARD

4 BUTTON MUSHROOMS, STEMS REMOVED, FINELY CHOPPED

¼ POUND HAVART WITH DILL CHEESE, CUT INTO ¼-INCH PIECES

SALT AND PEPPER

EXTRA VIRGIN OLIVE OIL, FOR DRIZZLING, PLUS A COUPLE TABLESPOONS

1 CUP SOUR CREAM

3 TO 4 TABLESPOONS FRESH DILL, CHOPPED OR SNIPPED WITH KITCHEN SCISSORS

3 TO 4 TABLESPOONS CAPERS, DRAINED — RUN YOUR KNIFE THROUGH THEM ONCE (OPTIONAL)

1 SEEDLESS CUCUMBER, CUT INTO ½ LENGTHWISE, THEN SLICED INTO HALF MOONS

1 SMALL RED ONION, PEELED AND SLICED

3 PLUM TOMATOES, SEEDED THEN THINLY SLICED

1-POUND WASHED BABY SPINACH LEAVES

2 TABLESPOONS WHITE VINEGAR

4 CRUSTY POPPY SEED ROLLS OR OTHER BURGER BUNS OF CHOICE (I FIND IT IMPORTANT TO BUY GREAT QUALITY BUNS AS IT REALLY DOESN'T MAKE SENSE TO MAKE A FABULOUS BURGER AND RUIN IT WITH A CHEAP BUN)

2 LARGE RADISHES, THINLY SLICED

1 SACK GOURMET POTATO CHIPS, SUCH AS TERRA CHIPS ONION AND HERB YUKON GOLD OR BLUE POTATO CHIPS

Combine ground chicken, poultry seasoning, chopped shallots, Dijon mustard, chopped mushroom, diced Havarti, salt and pepper, and a drizzle of extra-virgin olive oil. Mix thoroughly. Score the meat with your hand marking 4 equal portions. Form each portion into large 1-inch thick patties.

Preheat a nonstick skillet over medium-high heat. Drizzle extra-virgin olive oil over the patties and place them in the hot skillet. Cook 5 minutes per side until the patties are firm to the touch and cooked through.

While the burgers are cooking, prepare the herb caper sauce and mod salad. In a small bowl, combine the sour cream, chopped dill and capers then season with salt and pepper.

In a salad bowl combine the cucumbers, half of the red onion, plum tomatoes and 3/4 sack of baby spinach. Dress the salad with white vinegar, salt and pepper then drizzle with a couple tablespoons extra-virgin olive oil to coat the salad lightly and evenly. Toss to combine and adjust salt and pepper, to your taste.

Split the rolls or buns. Place the burgers on the bun bottoms. Top with sliced radishes, baby spinach and a heaping spoonful of herb-caper dressing slathered across the bun tops. Add remaining sauce into the salad and combine to give your salad a creamy finish. Fancy chips finish the plate.

Dessert

Danish Oatmeal Cookies

INGREDIENTS

1 CUP ALL-PURPOSE FLOUR

½ TEASPOON BAKING SODA

¼ TEASPOON SALT

1 CUP BUTTER, SOFTENED

1 CUP, CONFECTIONERS' SUGAR

2 TEASPOONS VANILLA EXTRACT

1 CUP OATMEAL

1 CUP CHOPPED PECANS (OPTIONAL)

1 TABLESPOON CONFECTIONERS' SUGAR OR AS NEEDED

Preheat an oven to 325 degrees F. Line a baking sheet with parchment paper.

In a bowl, mix the flour, baking soda, and salt. Once all dry ingredients are mixed, start the wet ingredients. In a separate large bowl, mix the butter, 1 cup confectioners' sugar, and vanilla until the mixture is smooth and creamy.

Stir in the flour mixture; gently stir in the oatmeal and pecans and lightly mix until combined.

With a spoon, drop about 1 scant tablespoon of dough per cookie onto the prepared baking sheet. Bake in the preheated oven until lightly browned, about 20 minutes. Let cool completely before sprinkling cookies with confectioners' sugar.

EGYPT

Dedra's Notes

Egypt is a very special country indeed. I didn't enjoy it enough the first time, so I had to go twice, and even that's not enough. There's no country that offers more in terms of wonders of the Ancient world, something that has interested me always. The Sphinx and the Egyptian Museum in particular were sights that I'll always treasure. I've looked at the mummy of Ramses II and I've ridden on a camel between the Pyramids of Giza, memories that are etched in my mind for all time as the hieroglyphics on the walls of the ancient tombs.

Egyptians are all about enjoying life, and that includes enjoying the tastiest food. Calories are not something that they concern themselves with, only taste and enjoying it with a big family or a group of friends. This country will always have a special place in my heart.

Menu

Starter

Falafel (Vegan)

Entree

Egyptian Koshari

– or –

Egyptian Kebabs

Dessert

Om Ali

Starter

Falafel

INGREDIENTS

1 (16 OUNCE) CANS CHICKPEAS OR 1 (16 OUNCE) CANS GARBANZO BEANS
1 LARGE ONION, CHOPPED
2 GARLIC CLOVES, CHOPPED
1 TEASPOON CORIANDER
1 TEASPOON CUMIN
½ TEASPOON BAKING POWDER
½ TEASPOON SALT
¼ TEASPOON PEPPER
2 CUPS OIL (FOR FRYING)

Place all ingredients except frying oil in a food processor and process to a thick chunky paste.

Form the mixture into small balls, about the size of a ping pong ball. Make sure they are nice and plump, and as perfectly round as you can make them.

Fry in 2 inches of hot oil until golden brown, about 5-7 minutes.

Serve hot in pita pockets or any flat bread, along with lettuce and tomatoes, and top with yogurt or tahini. My kids also love them as snacks, since they are crunchy and easily portable.

Entree

Koshari

Heat 1 tablespoon vegetable oil in a saucepan over medium-high heat. Stir in rice; continue stirring until rice is coated with oil, about 3 minutes. Add 3 cups water and 1 teaspoon of salt. Bring to a boil; reduce heat to low, cover, and simmer until the rice is tender and liquid has been absorbed, 20 to 25 minutes.

Fill a large pot with lightly salted water and bring to a rolling boil over high heat. Stir in the macaroni, and return to a boil. Cook the macaroni uncovered, stirring occasionally, until the it has cooked through, but is still firm to the bite, about 8 minutes. Drain well in a colander.

Return macaroni to cooking pot, cover and keep warm.

Soak lentils for 30 minutes. Drain and rinse; drain again. Bring 2 cups water to a boil in a pot and stir in lentils. Bring to a boil; cover and reduce heat to low. Simmer until lentils are tender 15 or 20 minutes. Stir in 1/2 teaspoon salt.

Heat 1 tablespoon vegetable oil in a large skillet over medium-high heat. Cook the onions in the oil, stirring often, until they begin to brown, 10 to 15 minutes. Onions should be a nice caramelized brown color. Add garlic and cook another minute. Remove from pan, drain on a paper towel-lined plate.

Place half of the onion mixture into a saucepan. Mix in the vinegar. Add the chopped tomatoes and tomato paste, black pepper, 2 teaspoons salt, cumin, and cayenne (if using). Bring to a boil then reduce heat to medium-low and simmer about 12 minutes.

Serve by placing a spoonful of rice, then macaroni, and then the lentils on serving plates. Sprinkle with some of the browned onions, then top with tomato sauce. My vegan children love this recipe.

INGREDIENTS

1 TABLESPOON VEGETABLE OIL
2 CUPS UNCOOKED WHITE RICE
3 CUPS WATER
1 TEASPOON SALT
1 (16 OUNCE) PACKAGE UNCOOKED ELBOW MACARONI
1 CUP BROWN LENTILS, SOAKED IN WATER
½ TEASPOON SALT
1 TABLESPOON VEGETABLE OIL
5 ONIONS, MINCED
2 CLOVES, GARLIC, MINCED
3 TABLESPOONS DISTILLED IN WHITE VINEGAR
4 RIPE TOMATOES, DICED.
½ CUP TOMATO PASTE
1 TEASPOON SALT
1 TEASPOON GROUND BLACK PEPPER
2 ½ TEASPOONS GROUND CUMIN
¼ TEASPOON CAYENNE PEPPER

VEGAN FOOD

Entree

Egyptian Kebab

Egyptian Kebab is ideal for sharing with guests. It's not only flavorful, it's great looking also! Guests will be convinced that you've made something very complicated and impressive!

INGREDIENTS

3 BONELESS SKINLESS CHICKEN BREASTS
4 TABLESPOONS YOGURT
1/2 TEASPOON SALT
¼ TEASPOON TURMERIC
1/8 TEASPOON DRY MUSTARD
½ TEASPOON CURRY POWDER
1/8 TEASPOON GROUND CARDAMOM
1 TEASPOON LEMON JUICE
1 TEASPOON WHITE VINEGAR
1/2 ONION, CUT IN HALF AND BROKEN UP INTO LAYERS
4 SMALL TOMATOES, HALVED.
8 BAMBOO SKEWERS
1 LEMON, CUT IN WEDGES
PARSLEY

Cut chicken breasts into 1 inch cubes, 16 in total.

Combine the yogurt, salt, turmeric, mustard, curry powder, cardamom, lemon juice and vinegar in a non-reactive bowl. Add chicken cubes and let sit in fridge 30-45 minutes.

Soak skewers in water.

Thread chicken, onions and tomatoes onto skewers alternating as follows: Chicken-Onion-Chicken-Onion-Tomato-Onion-Chicken-Onion-Chicken-Onion.

Grill or broil about 8-10 minutes, turning half way through cooking time.

Garnish with parsley and serve with lemon wedges for squeezing on top.

Dessert

Um Ali

INGREDIENTS

1 (17.5 OUNCE) PACKAGE FROZEN PUFF PASTRY
SHEETS, THAWED

3/4 CUP CHOPPED WALNUTS

1 CUP CHOPPED PECANS

1 CUP CHOPPED HAZELNUTS

1/2 CUP RAISINS

1 CUP FLAKED COCONUT

1 1/4 CUPS WHITE SUGAR, DIVIDED

4 CUPS MILK

1/2 CUP HEAVY CREAM

Preheat oven to 350 degrees F (175 degrees C). Butter a 9x13-inch baking dish.

Place the pastry sheets in the baking dish and place the dish in the oven. Watch it closely. When the top layer turns crunchy and golden, remove it from the oven. Continue until all the sheets are cooked.

Preheat the oven's broiler.

In a bowl, combine walnuts, pecans, hazelnuts, raisins, coconut and 1/4 cup sugar. Break cooked pastry into pieces and stir into nut mixture. Spread mixture evenly in 9x13-inch dish.

Bring milk and 1/2 cup sugar to a boil in a medium saucepan over medium heat. Pour over nut mixture.

Beat the heavy cream with the remaining 1/2 cup sugar until stiff peaks form. Spread evenly over nut mixture in dish.

Place dessert under oven broiler until top is golden brown, about 10 minutes. Serve hot.

ENGLAND

THE LAND OF SHAKESPEARE

England has had a long standing friendship with the USA, and I always knew that it was only a matter of time before I'd go there to see it for myself. I've been fortunate enough to travel to England 4 times now, and I can tell you that Americans have a language in common with the English, and many of us look similar, but that's largely where the similarity ends. The cuisine is just one example of how different we really are, although the English do enjoy meat and potatoes as well as fried foods, just like Americans. The Shepard's Pie recipe I've included is usually made with Beef and Cheese, but I prepared it as a "vegan" version for my family. If you want to make it as the classic recipe, simply substitute vegan meat and Soy Cheese with real Beef, Mayo and Cheese.

Menu

Starter

Prawn Cocktail

Entree

Fish and Chips

– or –

Vegan Shepherd's Pie

Dessert

Chocolate Chip Scones

Starter

Prawn Cocktail

INGREDIENTS

500G (2 CUPS) PEELED, COOKED PRAWNS OR SHRIMP

4 TABLESPOONS MAYONNAISE

1 TABLESPOON CREAMED HORSERADISH SAUCE

1 TABLESPOON TOMATO KETCHUP

2 CUPS SHREDDED ROMAINE OR ICEBERG LETTUCE

1 LIME, QUARTERED

4 LARGE, COOKED PRAWNS, SHELLED WITH TAIL ON (OPTIONAL)

MEDIUM PRAWNS CAN BE USED AS WELL, AND ARRANGED IN ANY WAY THAT YOU WISH.

Place the prawns into a large bowl. Add the Mayonnaise, creamed horseradish and tomato ketchup and stir to combine all the ingredients. Make sure all the prawns or shrimp are coated in the sauce if it seems a little thin, add a little more of each sauce ingredient.

Divide the shredded lettuce between 4 large wine glasses and top with the prawns and sauce. Arrange in a neat pile, not only slap on the top.

Decorate each glass with a wedge of lime and place a large prawn on the edge of the glass (if using) and serve immediately with small slices of buttered brown bread. If you are not serving the cocktail immediately, then assemble the sauce and keep in the fridge with the prawns and put together at the last minute. If you make the cocktail too far in advance, it tends to become watery and not so nice to eat. Make sure you mix it together just before you want to serve it.

Entree

Fish and Chips

INGREDIENTS

4 LARGE POTATOES, PEELED AND CUT INTO STRIPS
1 CUP ALL-PURPOSE FLOUR
1 TEASPOON BAKING POWDER
1 TEASPOON SALT
1 TEASPOON GROUND BLACK PEPPER
1 CUP MILK
1 EGG
1-QUART VEGETABLE OIL FOR FRYING
1 1/2 TO 2 POUNDS COD FILLETS

Place potatoes in a medium-size bowl of cold water. In a separate medium-size mixing bowl, mix together flour, baking powder, salt, and pepper. Stir in the milk and egg; stir until the mixture is smooth. Let mixture stand for 20 minutes.

Preheat the oil in a large pot or a deep fryer.

Fry the potatoes in the hot oil until they are tender. Drain them on paper towels.

Dredge the fish in the batter, one piece at a time, and place them in the hot oil. Fry until the fish is golden brown. If necessary, increase the heat to maintain 350 degrees F (175 degrees C) temperature. Drain well on paper towels. Make sure the breading is very crispy.

You can fry the potatoes again for 1 to 2 minutes for added crispness.

Ideally, this is served with mushy green peas. I tried it, and my family loved it, but I must warn you that this dish is VERY calorific.

Entree

Shepherd's Pie

INGREDIENTS

TO MAKE THE MASHED POTATO LAYER:

5 RUSSET POTATOES, PEELED AND CUT INTO 1-INCH CUBES
1/2 CUP VEGAN MAYONNAISE
1/2 CUP SOY MILK
1/4 CUP OLIVE OIL
3 TABLESPOONS VEGAN CREAM CHEESE SUBSTITUTE (AVAILABLE IN MOST HEALTH FOOD SUPERMARKETS)
2 TEASPOONS SALT

TO PREPARE THE BOTTOM LAYER:

1 TABLESPOON VEGETABLE OIL
1 LARGE ONION, CHOPPED
2 CARROTS, CHOPPED
3 STALKS CELERY, CHOPPED
1/2 CUP FROZEN PEAS
1 TOMATO, CHOPPED
½ TEASPOON OREGANO
½ TEASPOON CORIANDER
½ TEASPOON BASIL
2 CLOVES GARLIC, MINCED, OR MORE TO TASTE
1 PINCH GROUND BLACK PEPPER TO TASTE
1 (14 OUNCE) PACKAGE VEGETARIAN GROUND BEEF SUBSTITUTE (AVAILABLE IN MOST HEALTH FOOD SUPERMARKETS)
1/2 CUP SHREDDED CHEDDAR-STYLE SOY CHEESE (AVAILABLE IN MOST HEALTH FOOD SUPERMARKETS)

VEGAN FOOD

Place the potatoes in a pot, cover with cold water, and bring to a boil over medium-high heat.

Turn the heat to medium-low, and boil the potatoes until tender, about 25 minutes; drain.

Stir the vegan mayonnaise, soy milk, olive oil, vegan cream cheese, and salt into the potatoes, and mash with a potato masher until smooth and fluffy. Set the potatoes aside.

Preheat oven to 400 degrees F (200 degrees C), and spray a 2-quart baking dish with cooking spray.

Heat the vegetable oil in a large skillet over medium heat, and cook and stir the onion, carrots, celery, frozen peas, and tomato until softened, about 10 minutes. Stir in all the seasonings, garlic, and pepper.

Reduce the heat to medium-low, and crumble the vegetarian ground beef substitute into the skillet with the vegetables. Cook and stir, breaking up the meat substitute, until the mixture is hot, about 5 minutes.

Spread the vegetarian meat substitute mixture into the bottom of the baking dish, and top with the mashed potatoes, smoothing them into an even layer. Sprinkle the potatoes with the shredded soy cheese.

Bake in the preheated oven until the cheese is melted and slightly browned and the casserole is hot, about 20 minutes.

Garnish with some slices veggies, thyme leaves, or sprigs of parsley.

Dessert

Chocolate Chips Scones

INGREDIENTS

2 CUPS UNBLEACHED ALL-PURPOSE FLOUR
1/3 CUP PLUS 2 TABLESPOONS SUGAR
1 TEASPOON BAKING POWDER
1/2 TEASPOON BAKING SODA
1/2 TEASPOON SALT
6 TABLESPOONS (3/4 STICK) CHILLED UNSALTED BUTTER, DICED
1 TEASPOON (PACKED) GRATED LEMON PEEL
3/4 CUP MINIATURE SEMISWEET CHOCOLATE CHIPS
3/4 CUP CHILLED BUTTERMILK (IN UAE, WE DON'T HAVE BUTTERMILK AVAILABLE MOST OF THE TIME, SO I WOULD USE ¾ CUP OF MILK MIXED WITH A TABLESPOON OF LEMON JUICE THAT'S LEFT TO SIT FOR 5 MINUTES)
1 LARGE EGG YOLK
1 TEASPOON VANILLA EXTRACT
MILK (FOR GLAZE)

Butter and flour baking sheet.

Sift 2 cups flour, 1/3 cup sugar, baking powder, baking soda and salt into large bowl.

Add butter and lemon peel; rub in with fingertips until butter is reduced to size of rice grains.

Mix in chocolate chips.

Whisk buttermilk, egg yolk and vanilla in small bowl to blend.

Add buttermilk mixture to dry ingredients; mix until dough comes together in moist clumps.

Gather dough into ball. Form small balls with the dough, roughly 6 or 7, and place them at least 2 inches apart on the cookie sheet. (Can be prepared 1 day ahead. Just cover and refrigerate if you wish to do this.)

Preheat oven to 400°. Brush scones lightly with milk; sprinkle with remaining 2 tablespoons sugar. Bake until scones are crusty on top and knife inserted into center comes out clean, about 20 minutes. Serve warm.

FRANCE

THE LAND OF LOVE AND BEAUTY

Ah Paris! I had the extreme pleasure of visiting Paris once, and it was delightful from beginning to end. When I saw the Eiffel Tower for the first time, I shrieked in delight, as though I had just seen a celebrity. Everything about Paris was glamorous and beautiful, and it's impossible to take a bad picture there, as each angle produces an amazing shot, each and every time. The French want everything to be beautiful, special and very perfect, and this careful attention to detail spills through into their cuisine. One cannot help but admire this in the French, this pride in their work and in their customs. When I prepare French food, I can't help but feel as they do, that it should be beautiful and perfect, and although the portions are small, the taste is to die for.

Menu

Starter

Chicken Cordon Bleu

Entree

Ratatouille
– or –
Filet Mignon with Pepper Cream Sauce

Dessert

Banana Soufflé

Starter

Cordon Bleu Chicken Rolls

INGREDIENTS

8 SKINLESS, BONELESS CHICKEN BREASTS
8 SLICES COOKED TURKEY HAM
4 SLICES SWISS CHEESE, CUT INTO 1 INCH PIECES
SALT AND PEPPER TO TASTE
1 TEASPOON DRIED THYME
¼ CUP MELTED BUTTER
½ CUP CORN FLAKES CEREAL CRUMBS
1 (10.75 OUNCE) CAN CONDENSED CREAM OF
CHICKEN SOUP
½ CUP SOUR CREAM
1 TEASPOON LEMON JUICE

Preheat oven to 400 degrees F (200 degrees C).

Place each chicken breast half between sheets of plastic wrap and pound with a meat mallet to about 1/8-inch thickness.

Place a finger of cheese on each Turkey ham slice and sprinkle lightly with thyme and salt and pepper to taste. Roll up seasoned Turkey ham and cheese 'jelly roll style', then roll each chicken breast with ham and cheese inside. Tuck in ends and fasten with toothpicks.

Place melted butter in a small bowl and place cereal crumbs in a shallow dish or bowl. Dip each chicken roll in butter or margarine, then roll in crumbs, turning to coat thoroughly. Place coated rolls in a lightly greased 9x13 inch baking dish.

Bake at 400 degrees F (200 degrees C) for about 40 minutes or until chicken is golden brown and juices run clear. Serve with cordon bleu sauce, if desired.

To Make Cordon Bleu Sauce: In a small saucepan mix together the soup, sour cream and lemon juice. Heat over low heat, stirring occasionally, and serve hot over chicken rolls.

Entree

Ratatouille

INGREDIENTS

2 TABLESPOONS OLIVE OIL
3 CLOVES GARLIC, MINCED
2 TEASPOONS DRIED PARSLEY
1 EGGPLANT, CUT INTO ½ INCH CUBES
SALT TO TASTE
1 CUP GRATED PARMESAN CHEESE (CAN USE SOY
CHEESE TO MAKE THIS VEGAN)
2 ZUCCHINI, SLICED
1 LARGE ONION, SLICED INTO RINGS
2 CUPS SLICED FRESH MUSHROOMS
1 GREEN BELL PEPPER, SLICED
2 LARGE TOMATOES, CHOPPED

Preheat oven to 350 degrees F (175 degrees C). Coat bottom and sides of a 1 1/2-quart casserole dish with 1 tablespoon olive oil.

Heat remaining 1 tablespoon olive oil in a medium skillet over medium heat. Cook and stir garlic until lightly browned. Mix in parsley and eggplant. Cook and stir until eggplant is soft, about 10 minutes. Season with salt to taste.

Spread eggplant mixture evenly across bottom of prepared casserole dish. Sprinkle with a few tablespoons of Parmesan cheese. Spread zucchini in an even layer over top. Be as decorative as possible, as this is French cooking and presentation is everything.

Lightly salt and sprinkle with a little more cheese. Continue layering in this fashion, with onion, mushrooms, bell pepper, and tomatoes, covering each layer with a sprinkling of salt and cheese.

Bake in preheated oven for 45 minutes.

Entree

Filet Mignon with Pepper Cream Sauce

INGREDIENTS

¼ CUP COARSELY CRUSHED BLACK PEPPERCORNS

4 (6 OUNCE) 1 ½ INCH THICK FILET MIGNON STEAKS

SALT TO TASTE

1 TABLESPOON BUTTER

1 TEASPOON OLIVE OIL

1/3 CUP BEEF BROTH (YOU CAN USE VEGETABLE
BROTH AS LONG AS IT'S NOT TOO THIN)

1 CUP HEAVY CREAM

Place the peppercorns into a shallow bowl. Sprinkle the beef tenderloin filets with salt on both sides, and coat both sides with crushed peppercorns.

Melt the butter with the olive oil over high heat in a heavy skillet (not nonstick) until the foam disappears from the butter. Gently place the steaks in the pan, and cook until they start to become firm and are reddish-pink and juicy in the center, about 3 1/2 minutes per side, just seared on each side. An instant-read thermometer (if you have one) inserted into the center should read 130 degrees F (54 degrees C). Remove the steaks to platter, and cover tightly with foil.

Pour the beef broth into the skillet, and use a whisk to stir the broth and scrape up any dissolved brown flavor bits from the skillet. Whisk in the cream, and simmer the sauce until it's reduced and thickened, 6 to 7 minutes. Place the steaks back in the skillet, turn to coat with sauce, and serve with the remaining sauce.

Serve with some sautéed green beans or mashed potato.

Dessert

Banana Soufflé

INGREDIENTS

1 TABLESPOON UNSALTED BUTTER, MELTED
2 TEASPOONS WHITE SUGAR
2 EGG WHITES
2 EGGS, SEPARATED
1 PINCH SALT
2 RIPE BANANAS, MASHED
1 TABLESPOON HONEY, OR MORE TO TASTE
½ TEASPOON VANILLA EXTRACT
½ TEASPOON GRATED FRESH GINGER ROOT
1 TABLESPOON SWEETENED COCOA POWDER

Preheat oven to 400 degrees F (200 degrees C). Brush 4 1-cup soufflé dishes with melted butter; sprinkle the insides of the cups with sugar.

Set the egg yolks aside, and place the 4 egg whites into the work bowl of an electric mixer. Beat the egg whites and salt until the whites form soft peaks.

Place the 2 egg yolks, bananas, honey, vanilla extract, and ginger into a blender; pulse until smooth.

Scoop the banana mixture into a bowl; use a rubber spatula or wire whisk to gently fold 1/4 of the beaten egg whites into the banana mixture. Gently run the spatula through the center of the bowl, then around the sides of the bowl, repeating until fully incorporated. Fold in the remaining egg whites, being careful to keep as much air in the mixture as possible. I found the fluffiness of this to be wonderful, but don't touch it or it will deflate.

Spoon the soufflé mixture into the prepared dishes; bake in the preheated oven until the soufflés have puffed up above the baking dishes and the tops are browned, about 15 minutes.

Sift a little sweetened cocoa powder over each soufflé for garnish to serve.

GERMANY

THE LAND OF IDEAS

I've not had the pleasure of visiting Germany, but I've got it on my list. Thankfully, my eldest son has been, and he had nothing but wonderful things to say about his experiences. The people have so much to teach us, and the history of Germany is one of resilience. Time and time again, this country has proven their strength, as they've fallen and pulled themselves back to excellence over and over. Germans are known for inventiveness, and this extends to their cuisine.

Menu

Starter

German Potato Salad

Entree

Zwiebelkuchen (German Onion Pie)

– or –

Jagerschnitzel

Dessert

One Bowl Vegan Chocolate Cake

Starter

German Potato Salad

INGREDIENTS

3 CUPS DICED PEELED POTATOES

4 SLICES TURKEY BACON

1 SMALL ONION, DICED

¼ CUP WHITE VINEGAR

2 TABLESPOONS WATER

3 TABLESPOONS WHITE SUGAR

1 TEASPOON SALT

1/8 TEASPOON GROUND BLACK PEPPER

1 TABLESPOON CHOPPED FRESH PARSLEY

Place the potatoes into a pot, and fill with enough water to cover.

Bring to a boil, and cook for about 10 minutes, or until easily pierced with a fork.

Drain, and set aside to cool.

Place the bacon in a large deep skillet over medium-high heat. Fry until browned and crisp, turning as needed. Remove from the pan and set aside.

Add onion to the bacon grease, and cook over medium heat until browned. Add the vinegar, water, sugar, salt and pepper to the pan.

Bring to a boil, then add the potatoes and parsley. Crumble in half of the bacon. Heat through, then transfer to a serving dish. Crumble the remaining bacon over the top, and serve warm.

Entree

German Onion Pie

To make the pastry:

Combine the flour, salt and cornstarch in a food processor and pulse once or twice to mix. Add the margarine a couple of tablespoons at a time and process until the mixture looks like rough breadcrumbs. Then add the canola oil and soy milk (1 tablespoon at a time) until the mixture clumps together as you process it (you may need to add more soy milk if the consistency isn't reached).

If you don't have a food processor: combine the dry ingredients and then rub the margarine through the dry ingredients with your fingertips until it reaches a breadcrumbs consistency.

Add the wet ingredients and knead with your hands until the dough sticks together in a ball, but doesn't stick to your fingers.

Flatten the dough out into a disk, wrap in plastic and refrigerate for an hour.

Preheat the oven to 160 degrees.

Roll out the pastry (it is a fairly crumbly pastry so it is a little difficult to work with, but don't worry you can fix it up with minimal problems) about ½ cm thick and lay it out on a greased pie or quiche dish. Patch up any gaps or holes by pressing pieces of rolled dough into it. Don't worry it doesn't need to look perfect.

Prick the base with a fork and bake for 20 minutes.

NOTE: After you remove the crust from the oven increase the temperature to 180 degrees.

To make the filling:

Heat the olive oil in a large pan and sauté the onions until lightly golden and cooked. Place in a mixing bowl.

Drain the cashews (which have been soaking) and place in a food processor with the lemon juice (a small one will work best) –if you have a mini one like a magic bullet then use this and then transfer to a larger processor for the rest of the filling ingredients) and process until they form a smooth paste (you will likely need to scrape the sides a lot.

Add the tofu, garlic and arrowroot to the filling and process until all smooth.

Add this mixture to the bowl with the onions in it along the oregano, caraway seeds, flour and salt and pepper to taste. Mix well.

Pour the filling into the baked pie crust and smooth the top over as much as you can.

Bake at 100 degrees Celsius for 20 minutes.

INGREDIENTS

THE PASTRY BASE:
1 ½ CUPS WHOLEMEAL FLOUR
½ TEASPOON SALT
1 TABLESPOON CORNSTARCH
9 TABLESPOONS VEGAN MARGARINE
1 ½ TEASPOONS CANOLA OIL
4 TABLESPOONS SOY MILK

THE FILLING:
5 BIG ONIONS, PEELED AND SLICED
2 TABLESPOONS OLIVE OIL
¼ CUP CASHEWS, SOAKED ON COLD WATER FOR AN HOUR OR MORE
300G SILKEN TOFU
1 TABLESPOON LEMON JUICE
1 CLOVE GARLIC, CRUSHED
2 TABLESPOONS ARROWROOT
1 TABLESPOON CHOPPED OREGANO (OR THYME)
1 TEASPOON CARAWAY SEEDS
1 TABLESPOON FLOUR

VEGAN FOOD

Entree

Jagerschnitzel

INGREDIENTS

1 CUP BREAD CRUMBS
1 TABLESPOON ALL-PURPOSE FLOUR
SALT AND PEPPER TO TASTE
2 TABLESPOONS VEGETABLE OIL
4 BEEF STEAKS OR CUTLETS, POUNDED THIN
1 EGG, BEATEN
1 MEDIUM ONION, DICED
1 (8 OUNCE) CAN SLICED MUSHROOMS
1 ½ CUPS WATER
1 CUBE BEEF OR VEGETABLE BOUILLON
1 TABLESPOON CORNSTARCH
½ CUP SOUR CREAM

In a shallow dish, mix together the bread crumbs and flour. Season with salt and pepper. Place the egg in a separate dish. Heat oil in a large skillet over medium-high heat. Dip steaks in egg, then coat with the bread crumb mixture. Fry in the hot oil until browned on both sides and cooked through, about 5 minutes per side.

Remove the steak to a platter and keep warm. Add onion and mushrooms to the skillet and cook until lightly browned. Pour in water and dissolve the bouillon cube. Simmer for about 20 minutes. Stir together the cornstarch and sour cream; stir into the skillet. Cook over low heat until thickened but do not boil. Spoon over the beef cutlets and serve immediately.

Dessert

One Bowl Vegan Chocolate Cake

VEGAN FOOD

Preheat oven to 350 degrees F (176 C) and lightly spray (2) 8-inch round cake pans or 1 large rectangular pan with nonstick spray (see notes for cooking times for different size pans). Dust with cocoa powder, shake out the excess and set aside.

Mix the almond milk and vinegar in a large mixing bowl, and let set for a few minutes to activate. Add the oil, coffee, vanilla extract, and applesauce and beat until foamy.

Add the flour, sugar, cocoa powder, baking soda, baking powder, and salt to a sifter and slowly sift over the wet ingredients while mixing with a hand-held or standing mixer. If you don't have a sifter, simply mix dry ingredients in another bowl and add to the wet mixture while beating.

Beat until no large lumps remain. It should be creamy and pourable. Taste and adjust sweetness as needed, adding more sugar if desired (I found that this was just fine).

Divide batter evenly between your 2 cake pans or rectangular pan.

Bake 25-30 minutes, or until a toothpick inserted into the center comes out clean. Let cool completely before frosting.

While cooling, prepare frosting by beating together all ingredients until light and fluffy, adding the powdered sugar in small amounts until you reach your desired consistency and sweetness. If it becomes too thick, add more almond milk. If it's too thin, add more cocoa powder or powdered sugar.

Once the cake is cooled, frost generously with buttercream frosting, adding a thick layer between the top and bottom layers (if doing a 2-layer cake). Alternatively, omit the frosting and dust with cocoa powder.

Serve with a scoop of dairy-free ice cream, a drizzle of chocolate, or caramel sauce, coconut whipped cream or a glass of almond milk!

My Vegan son LOVED this cake! One of his favorites.

INGREDIENTS

CAKE:
1 ½ CUPS (360 ML) ORIGINAL UNSWEETENED ALMOND MILK
2 TSP WHITE OR APPLE CIDER VINEGAR
1 ¼ CUPS (307 G) UNSWEETENED APPLESAUCE*
½ CUP (120 ML) STRONG BREWED COFFEE (OR SUB MORE ALMOND MILK)
2/3 CUP (160 ML) MELTED COCONUT OIL, OR SUB GRAPE SEED OR CANOLA OIL
2 TSP PURE VANILLA EXTRACT
2 CUPS + 2 TBSP. (320 G) WHOLE-WHEAT PASTRY FLOUR OR UNBLEACHED ALL-PURPOSE FLOUR
1 1/3 CUPS (266 G) ORGANIC CANE SUGAR (OR SUB GRANULATED SUGAR)
1 CUP (96 G) UNSWEETENED COCOA POWDER
2 TSP BAKING SODA
1 TSP BAKING POWDER
¼ TSP SALT

FROSTING:
1 CUP (16 TBSP. OR 224 G) VEGAN BUTTER, SOFTENED
2 ½ - 3 CUPS (280-336 G) POWDERED SUGAR
2/3 CUP (63 G) UNSWEETENED COCOA POWDER
¼ CUP (30G) DAIRY-FREE SEMI SWEET CHOCOLATE, MELTED AND SLIGHTLY COOLED
2 TSP PURE VANILLA EXTRACT
¼ CUP UNSWEETENED ORIGINAL ALMOND MILK

GREECE

THE LAND OF ANCIENT BEAUTY AND WISDOM

Dedra's Notes

With deep regret, I admit that I haven't been to Greece, even though I have desperately wished to go. Preparing this chapter on Greek food made me long to go, and so one day I absolutely must! The beauty and attention to detail don't just apply to the architecture or artistic expression. The passion of the Greek is also communicated through the amazingly delicious food, which, by the way, is my personal favorite!

Menu

Starter

Traditional Gyros

Entree

Vegetarian Casserole (Vegan)

– or –

Moussaka

Dessert

Greek Lemon Cake

Starter

Traditional Gyros

INGREDIENTS

1 SMALL ONION, CUT INTO CHUNKS
1-POUND GROUND LAMB
1-POUND GROUND BEEF
1 TABLESPOON MINCED GARLIC
1 TEASPOON DRIED OREGANO
1 TEASPOON GROUND CUMIN
1 TEASPOON DRIED MARJORAM
1 TEASPOON DRIED THYME
1 TEASPOON DRIED ROSEMARY
1 TEASPOON FRESHLY GROUND BLACK PEPPER
¼ TEASPOON SEA SALT
BOILING WATER AS NEEDED
12 TABLESPOONS HUMMUS
12 PITA BREAD ROUNDS
1 SMALL HEAD LETTUCE, SHREDDED
1 LARGE TOMATO, SLICED
1 LARGE RED ONION, SLICED
6 OUNCES CRUMBLED FETA CHEESE
24 TABLESPOONS TZATZIKI SAUCE (IF YOU CAN'T FIND THIS, JUST MIX UP SOME MAYO, LEMON JUICE AND DILL)

Place onion in a food processor and blend until finely chopped. Transfer onion to a piece of cheese cloth and squeeze out the liquid. Place onion in a large bowl.

Mix lamb, beef, garlic, oregano, cumin, marjoram, thyme, rosemary, black pepper, and salt with the onion using your hands until well mixed. Cover bowl with plastic wrap and refrigerate until flavors combine, about an hour and a half.

Preheat oven to 325 degrees F (165 degrees C).

Place meat mixture in a food processor and pulse until finely chopped and course, about 1 minute. Pack meat mixture into a 7x4-inch loaf pan, ensuring there are no air pockets. Place loaf pan into a roasting pan and pour enough boiling water around the loaf pan to reach halfway up the sides.

Bake in the preheated oven until no longer pink in the center, 45 to 60 minutes. An instant-read thermometer inserted into the center should read at least 165 degrees F (74 degrees C). Pour off any accumulated fat and cool slightly.

Thinly slice the gyro meat mixture.

Spread 1 tablespoon hummus onto each pita bread; top each with gyro meat mixture, lettuce, tomato, red onion, feta cheese, and tzatziki sauce.

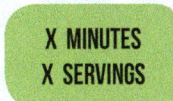
Entree

Greek Vegan Casserole

INGREDIENTS

8 LARGE EGGPLANTS
8 LARGE POTATOES
8 GREEN BELL PEPPERS
8 LARGE ONIONS
8 SUMMER SQUASH
6 TOMATOES
1 POUND FRESH GREEN BEANS
1 CUP BROCCOLI CHOPPED
1 POUND WHOLE FRESH MUSHROOMS
2 BULBS GARLIC, CLOVES SEPARATED AND PEELED
¼ CUP CHOPPED FRESH DILL WEED
¼ CUP CHOPPED FRESH OREGANO
¼ CUP CHOPPED FRESH BASIL
1 (15 OUNCE) CAN TOMATO SAUCE
¾ CUP OLIVE OIL
SALT AND PEPPER TO TASTE.

VEGAN FOOD

Prepare the eggplant before assembling ingredients, by cutting them into 2 inch chunks and putting them into an extra-large bowl with salted water to cover. This will draw out the bitterness from the eggplant. Let this sit for about 2 hours.

Preheat oven to 375 degrees F (190 degrees C).

Cut the potatoes, green bell peppers, onion, squash and tomatoes into 2-inch chunks. Cut the green beans and mushrooms in half and peel the garlic cloves.

Drain and rinse the eggplant, then combine it with all the other chopped vegetables, the dill, oregano and basil and place all into a 3x13x18 inch roasting pan. Pour the tomato sauce and olive oil over all.

Bake at 375 degrees F (190 degrees C) for 2 ½ hours, adding a little water about halfway through cooking time to keep moist.

Moussaka

INGREDIENTS

3 EGGPLANTS, PEELED AND CUT LENGTHWISE INTO
½ INCH THICK SLICES

SALT

¼ CUP OLIVE OIL

1 TABLESPOON BUTTER

1-POUND LEAN GROUND BEEF

SALT TO TASTE

GROUND BLACK PEPPER TO TASTE

2 ONIONS, CHOPPED

1 CLOVE GARLIC, MINCED

¼ TEASPOON GROUND CINNAMON

¼ TEASPOON GROUND NUTMEG

½ TEASPOON FINES HERBS

2 TABLESPOONS DRIED PARSLEY

1 (8 OUNCE) CAN TOMATO SAUCE

¼ CUP RED GRAPE VINEGAR

1 EGG, BEATEN

4 CUPS MILK

½ CUP BUTTER

6 TABLESPOONS ALL-PURPOSE FLOUR

SALT TO TASTE

GROUND WHITE PEPPER TO TASTE

1 ½ CUPS FRESHLY GRATED PARMESAN CHEESE

¼ TEASPOON GROUND NUTMEG

Lay the slices of eggplant on paper towels, sprinkle lightly with salt, and set aside for 30 minutes to draw out the moisture. Then in a skillet over high heat, heat the olive oil. Quickly fry the eggplant until browned. Set aside on paper towels to drain.

In a large skillet over medium heat, melt the butter and add the ground beef, salt and pepper to taste, onions, and garlic. After the beef is browned, sprinkle in the cinnamon, nutmeg, fines herbs and parsley. Pour in the tomato sauce and wine, and mix well. Simmer for 20 minutes. Allow to cool, and then stir in beaten egg.

To make the béchamel sauce, begin by scalding the milk in a saucepan. Melt the butter in a large skillet over medium heat. Whisk in flour until smooth. Lower heat; gradually pour in the hot milk, whisking constantly until it thickens. Season with salt, and white pepper.

Arrange a layer of eggplant in a greased 9x13 inch baking dish. Cover eggplant with all of the meat mixture, and then sprinkle ½ cup of Parmesan cheese over the meat. Make it look neat and pretty. Cover with remaining eggplant, and sprinkle another ½ cup of cheese on top. Pour the béchamel sauce over the top, and sprinkle with the nutmeg. Sprinkle with the remaining cheese.

Bake for 1 hour at 350 degrees F (175 degrees C). Enjoy!

Dessert

Greek Lemon Cake

INGREDIENTS

3 CUPS CAKE FLOUR
1 TEASPOON BAKING SODA
1/4 TEASPOON SALT
6 EGGS, SEPARATED
2 CUPS WHITE SUGAR, DIVIDED
1 CUP BUTTER, SOFTENED
2 TEASPOONS GRATED LEMON ZEST
2 TABLESPOONS LEMON JUICE
1 CUP PLAIN WHOLE-MILK YOGURT

Preheat oven to 350 degrees F (175 degrees C). Grease one 10-inch tube pan.

Sift the flour, baking soda, and salt together. Set mixture aside.

In a large bowl, beat the egg whites until soft peaks form. Gradually add 1/2 cup of the sugar, beating until stiff glossy peaks form. Set aside.

Beat butter and remaining 1 1/2 cups sugar in a large bowl with an electric mixer until fluffy, 3 to 5 minutes. The mixture should be noticeably lighter in color.

Blend in egg yolks, lemon zest, and lemon juice. Add flour mixture alternately with the yogurt, mixing until combined. Gently fold in the egg whites and pour the batter into the prepared pan.

Bake in preheated oven until a tester inserted in the center comes out clean, 50 to 60 minutes.

Let cake cool in pan for 10 minutes, then turn out onto a rack to finish cooling. Serves 12. This is a lovely cake for dessert, a snack or breakfast.

ICELAND

Dedra's Notes

I visited Iceland in the winter, believe it or not! Yes, I was there right after spending New Year's Eve in Copenhagen. What a cold time! I loved having an excuse to wear all those sweaters, gloves and coats. I was so happy to be that cold for a change. Being from the Middle East, I never got the chance to wear winter clothes or enjoy anything about a culture that snows, so it was a pleasure for me. Icelandic people are so peaceful, and so lucky to be able to visit places like the Blue Lagoon Spa, which rests at the foot of a volcano! Perhaps that's why they were always smiling? Their food is incredibly healthy, and in fact, Icelandic people are regarded as some of the healthiest people on the planet! Until today, we enjoy many of the dishes I learned there.

Menu

Starter

Icelandic Vegetable and Oat Soup
& Potato Flatbread

Entree

Icelandic Salmon Grill
– or –
Icelandic Lamb Fricassee

Dessert

Icelandic Pepper Cookies

Starter

Vegetable and Oat Soup with Flatbread

INGREDIENTS
3 TO 4 TBS EXTRA-VIRGIN OLIVE OIL
1 SMALL YELLOW ONION FINELY CHOPPED
1 MEDIUM LEEKS TRIMMED AND SLICED
3 TO 4 GARLIC CLOVES MINCED
10 MUSHROOMS THINLY SLICED
3 TO 4 MEDIUM CARROTS CUT INTO ¼-INCH SLICES
6 TO 8 CUPS WATER OR LOW-SODIUM VEGETABLE BROTH
2 MEDIUM POTATOES DICED SMALL
2 CUPS CAULIFLOWER FLORETS
1 MEDIUM DRIED BAY LEAF
1/4 CUP OLD-FASHIONED ROLLED OATS
1 CUP FINELY CHOPPED KALE OPTIONAL (I WOULD RECOMMEND YOU USE IT)

FLATBREAD INGREDIENTS
3 1/4 CUPS ALL-PURPOSE FLOUR
2 ½ TEASPOONS BAKING POWDER
2 TEASPOONS SALT
1 ½ TABLESPOON SUGAR
2 MEDIUM POTATOES, PEELED AND BOILED
½ CUP PLAIN FULL FAT YOGHURT
1 ¼ CUPS MILK

Heat the olive oil in a large saucepan over medium heat.

Once heated, add the onions and leeks; cook for 5 to 6 minutes, until the onions are soft and transparent.

Add the garlic and mushrooms, then cook for an additional 2 to 3 minutes.

Add the carrots and sauté for 1 to 2 minutes, just until lightly fragrant, then cover with 6 cups of water.

Add the potatoes, cauliflower, and bay leaf and bring to a boil.

Reduce heat to low, cover, and cook at a simmer for upwards of 2 hours.

After two hours, mix in the oats and kale and continue cooking for 10 to 15 minutes.

Season with a few heavy pinches of sea salt and serve with fresh ground pepper.

Mix together flour, baking powder, salt and sugar in a large bowl.

Use a fork to mash the potatoes.

In a medium bowl whisk together mashed potatoes, yogurt and milk. Make a well in the center of the flour mixture and pour in the potato mixture. Use a spatula to gradually work the flour into the potato mix.

Mix until you have everything combined, no more. Dump the dough onto a clean work surface.

Knead the dough until it is just about firm and everything is combined. Add a little more flour or milk if necessary. Knead as little as possible to avoid the dough becoming elastic. The dough should be a little sticky. Cover with plastic wrap and let it rest four at least an hour.

Divide the dough in half and shape each half to about 7 x 3-inches. Place one ball of dough on a generously floured surface and top with more flour. Use a rolling pin to roll it out to about 24 x 10-inches. Cut 3 rounds using an 8-inch plate as your template. Save the scraps.

Repeat with the other dough ball. You should have 6 nice rounds.

Take the scraps, work them into a ball, roll it out and you should be able to cut at least one more round.

The traditional way to cook these is directly on the stove burner. In this case you heat the burner to medium high. Place a round on the burner and prick the top with a fork to avoid big bubbles forming. Cook for about a minute or two, until the bottom is brown. Flip and cook the other side until brown. Adjust the temperature so as not to burn the bread. In general, it takes about 2 minutes to cook each round. Your time may be different.

If you don't cook these directly on the stove, use a non-stick pan and follow the directions above.

Cover your stack of breads with a clean kitchen towel and serve them when they have cooled to just room temperature.

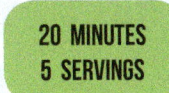

Entree

Icelandic Salmon Grill

INGREDIENTS

2 LARGE ONIONS, SLICED
BROWN SUGAR
BUTTER OR MARGARINE
SALT OR PEPPER
2 LBS WILD SALMON

Place two large pieces of tin foil down.

Spread sliced onion pieces from one onion, on tin foil the length of the salmon.

Lay salmon whole or fillet pieces on top of the onion slices.

Salt and pepper to taste

Lightly spread butter or margarine or salmon.

Sprinkle with your hand, brown sugar over salmon (Medium coverage).

Cover salmon with remaining onion slices.

Cover salmon with two pieces of tin foil and crimp sides together. Place on grill and check after about 10 minutes. Do not overcook the salmon. When the salmon changes color and can be flaked with a fork your fish is done.

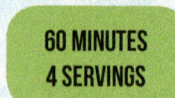
Entree

Icelandic Lamb Fricassee

INGREDIENTS

2 LB. LAMB

1 LB. WHITE CABBAGE

1 LB. CARROTS

1 LB. TURNIPS

4 C WATER

2 TEASPOONS SALT

¼ C MARGARINE

¼ C FLOUR

3 C LAMB BROTH

1 STALK CELERY, SLICED

Wash lamb and cut in small pieces.

Add salt to water and bring to a boil.

Add meat and cook, removing scrum for 25 minutes.

Wash Cabbage and break apart.

Wash and peel carrots and turnips and cut into quarters or smaller.

Cook with lamb until vegetables are tender.

Remove meat and vegetables to serving dish.

Melt Margarine.

Add Flour and blend.

Add broth, a little at a time, and cook, stirring constantly, until thickened.

Add finely sliced celery.

Pour sauce over lamb and Vegetables and its ready to serve.

Dessert

Icelandic Pepper Cookies

INGREDIENTS

1 1/4 CUPS BUTTER, SOFTENED
1 1/4 CUPS WHITE SUGAR
3/4 CUP LIGHT CORN SYRUP
2 SMALL EGGS
3 CUPS ALL-PURPOSE FLOUR
1 1/2 TEASPOONS BAKING POWDER
1 TEASPOON BAKING SODA
1/2 TEASPOON SALT
2 TEASPOONS GROUND CINNAMON
2 TEASPOONS GROUND CLOVES
1 TEASPOON GROUND GINGER
1/4 TEASPOON GROUND BLACK PEPPER

In a large bowl, cream butter and sugar. Stir in corn syrup and eggs; cream well. Sift together flour, baking powder, baking soda, salt, cinnamon, cloves, ginger, and pepper. Add dry ingredients to the butter mixture, and mix until smooth. Refrigerate dough overnight.

Preheat oven to 350 degrees F (175 degrees C).

Roll out dough to 1/4-inch thickness. Cut out cookies with a 2 inch round cookie cutter. Place at least 1 inch apart on cookie sheet and bake for 8 to 10 minutes in preheated oven.

INDIA

Dedra's Notes

In the UAE, we have many residents from India, so even though I've never been to India, I feel rather close to this culture, since it's everywhere here, especially in Sharjah where I live. We can literally pop around the corner and buy a large variety of Indian dishes, and they are all equally delicious! I must admit that I'm not very fond of their desserts, but managed to find something for this chapter. By the way, Indian food is very hot at its full strength, so you may want to adjust the spices to suit your own taste. I prefer to eat as the people of the nation do, and it's a great way to clear your nasal passages, but you may wish to adjust to suit your taste. There are also a lot of vegan choices in this one. Enjoy!

Menu

Starter

Paneer Tikka

Entree

Mushroom Soya Biryani

– or –

Aloo Broccoli Sabzi

Dessert

Avocado Chocolate Mousse

Starter

Paneer Tikka

Take a bowl and add curd, turmeric powder and chili powder; mix well.

Add to this add garlic paste, ginger paste, chaat masala powder and garam masala powder.

Later, add amchur (mango) powder, cumin powder; mix well.

Take finely chopped coriander and add it to this mixture.

Add 2 spoons of besan (gram or chickpea flour), which will help bind the batter well.

Add salt as per your preference, and squeeze in half a lemon to this.

Mix well.

Add the cut onion pieces, the red capsicum and green capsicum cubes.

Add paneer to this mixture.

Coat everything well and make sure all the onion, capsicum and paneer pieces are nicely coated.

Marinate it for 30 minutes.

Now, take the skewers and insert all these marinated pieces into it, again coat it evenly.

Heat the pan on a stove.

Add 1 spoon of oil and spread it over the pan.

Keep the skewers on top of it and allow it to be cooked.

Keep turning to be sure all sides are cooking.

Fry it until it turns golden brown in colour.

Remove the paneer, onion and capsicum pieces from the skewer.

Serve hot.

INGREDIENTS

PANEER - 1 PACK (CUT INTO CUBES)
CAPSICUM - 2 (1 GREEN CUT INTO SQUARE PIECES; 1 RED CUT INTO SQUARE PIECES)
CURD - 1 CUP
GINGER PASTE - ½ TSP
GARLIC PASTE - ½ TSP
TURMERIC POWDER - ½ TSP
CHILLI POWDER - ½ TSP
GRAM FLOUR - 2 ½ SPOONS
CUMIN POWDER - ½ TSP
AMCHUR POWDER (MANGO POWDER) - ½ TSP
GARAM MASALA POWDER - ½ TSP
LEMON JUICE - ½
CORIANDER - HALF CUP (FINELY CHOPPED)
CHAAT MASALA POWDER - 1 TSP
SALT - TO TASTE
ONION - 2 (CUT INTO SQUARE PIECES)
SKEWERS

Entree

Mushroom Soya Biryani

INGREDIENTS

1 LB. /1/2 KG MUSHROOM (CUT INTO SMALL PIECES)
1 CUP TOFU
2 CUPS BASMATI RICE
1 LARGE ONION (CUT LENGTHWISE)
2 FINELY CHOPPED OR CRUSHED TOMATOES
2 TEASPOONS OF GINGER GARLIC PASTE
¼ CUP OF FINELY CHOPPED CORIANDER LEAVES
¼ CUP OF FINELY CHOPPED MINT LEAVES
3 FINELY CHOPPED GREEN CHILIES
3 TABLESPOONS OF OIL
3 TABLESPOONS OF CRISCO OR BUTTER
½ CUP OF COCONUT MILK
3 CUPS OF WATER
2 TABLESPOONS OF YOGURT
SALT TO TASTE
2 TEASPOONS OF CHILI POWDER
2 TEASPOONS OF CORIANDER- CUMIN POWDER
½ TEASPOON OF FENNEL POWDER
¼ TEASPOON OF TURMERIC POWDER
WHOLE GRAM MASALA (1 BAY LEAF, 2 CINNAMON
STICKS, 5 CLOVES AND 3 CARDAMOM SEEDS.

Clean the mushroom with a wet kitchen towel to remove the dirt. Do not wash with water.

Cut it lengthwise to retain the mushroom shape.

Soak 2 cups of Basmati rice and the soya chunks separately.

In a heavy deep vessel heat oil and Crisco together and fry the whole gram masala (bay leaf, cinnamon, cloves, cardamom).

Add onions and sauté till golden brown. Slowly add chopped green chili, chopped coriander and mint leaves while sautéing the onions.

When onions turn slightly brown and crispy add ginger garlic paste and tomatoes and sauté till it becomes a paste.

Now add mushroom slices. Squeeze the water from the Tofu chunks and add it.

Add the turmeric powder, chili powder, coriander-cumin powder, fennel powder, yogurt, coconut milk and salt. Sauté everything until it thickens to a gravy consistency.

Drain all water from the rice and put it in a rice cooker. Add the gravy to the rice along with water and mix well. Check for Salt and switch on the rice cooker.

After the Biryani is done, gently fluff it up with a fork and garnish with coriander leaves. Serve hot with Raita and some side dish.

Entree

Aloo Broccoli Sabzi

INGREDIENTS

1 CROWN OF BROCCOLI (CUT INTO SMALL FLORETS)
2 OR 3 CHOPPED POTATOES
¼ TEASPOON TURMERIC POWDER
1 TEASPOON RED CHILI POWDER
¼ TEASPOON CUMIN POWDER
SALT TO TASTE

FOR SEASONING:
1 TABLESPOON OF OIL
¼ TEASPOON OF MUSTARD SEEDS
½ TEASPOON OF CUMIN (OR FENNEL) SEEDS

Wash the broccoli crown and chop it into small florets. You can use the stem of the broccoli spear also after peeling it.

Peel the potatoes, wash it and chop it into medium cubes roughly the same size as the broccoli florets.

Heat oil in the pan and add mustard seeds. When it begins to sputter, add the fennel seeds.

Add the chopped potatoes along with salt and pinch of turmeric.

Stir fry the potatoes in medium flame till they are half-cooked. You can cover with a lid for some time to cook it faster. Do not add water. I like to use a nonstick pan for this in order to reduce the amount of oil.

When the potatoes are partially cooked, add the broccoli florets. Stir fry in medium flame for 5 minutes till the broccoli turns dark green.

Now add the red chili powder and the cumin powder Reduce the heat and cook for another 2-3 minutes.

Dessert

Avocado Chocolate Mousse

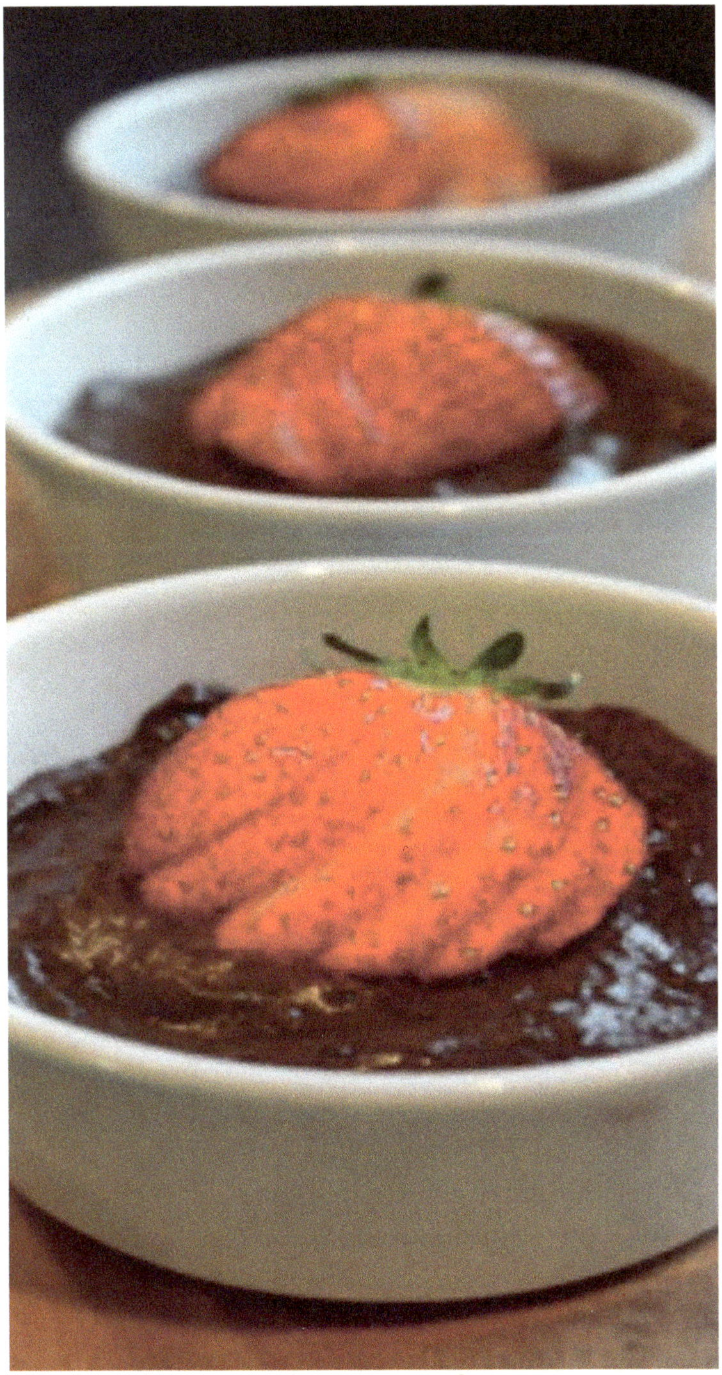

INGREDIENTS

1 LARGE AVOCADO (150-170G)
2 TBSP. COCOA POWDER
2 TBSP. MAPLE SYRUP/COCONUT SUGAR/
SUGAR
1 TSP VANILLA
3-4 STRAWBERRIES

Blend everything. Transfer to a bowl and chill for half an hour in the fridge before eating.

Garnish with sliced strawberries and enjoy!

INDONESIA

Dedra's Notes

Sadly, I've never had the chance to see Indonesia, but I've known many Indonesian people who've informed me that it's one of the most romantic places to visit, particularly Bali. Indonesia also has a rich ancient history with a stunning array of ancient temples throughout the country, each one with a brilliant folklore story to tell.

Ethnic diversity is vast and prior to the rise of Islam, between the 5th to 15th century, Dharmic faiths (Hinduism and Buddhism) were the majority in Indonesian archipelago, especially in Java and Sumatra.

Indonesian cuisine is very similar to Filipino cuisine, as it's sweet and savory at the same time, with a great deal of fresh tropical fruits and vegetables.

Menu

Starter

Charred Corn on the Cob

Entree

Sop Buntot

– or –

Indonesian Satay

Dessert

Banana Fritters

Starter

Charred Corn

INGREDIENTS

2 TABLESPOONS HONEY

1 TABLESPOON SALT

1/2 CUP MILK

6 CUPS COCONUT MILK

1/2 CUP BUTTER, MELTED

5 CORN ON THE COB, HUSKED

5 TABLESPOONS BUTTER

Stir together the honey, salt, milk, coconut milk, and melted butter. Add the corn, cover, and refrigerate overnight.

Preheat a charcoal grill for medium heat.

Remove corn from marinade and place each one on a skewer. Grill for 10 to 15 minutes until partially charred, baste occasionally with the coconut marinade as you grill. Serve with 1 tablespoon of butter per ear.

Entree

Sop Buntot (Indonesian Oxtail Soup)

INGREDIENTS

4 SHALLOTS, PEELED AND HALVED

1 LARGE ONION, QUARTERED, DIVIDED

1 (2 INCH) PIECE GINGER, PEELED AND THINLY SLICED ACROSS THE GRAIN

6 CLOVES GARLIC, PEELED

3 TABLESPOONS CANOLA OIL

1/2 TEASPOON GROUND NUTMEG

1/4 TEASPOON GROUND CINNAMON

4 POUNDS' MEATY OXTAIL PIECES, AT ROOM TEMPERATURE

2 LARGE CARROTS, CUT INTO 2-INCH PIECES

3 STALKS CELERY, CUT INTO 1-INCH PIECES

WATER TO COVER

2 TEASPOONS SALT

1/2 TEASPOON GROUND BLACK PEPPER

3 WAXY POTATOES, SCRUBBED AND CUT INTO 1 1/2-INCH CHUNKS

3 LARGE CARROTS, CUT INTO 2-INCH PIECES

2 TABLESPOONS WHITE SUGAR

2 TABLESPOONS FISH SAUCE

3 RIPE TOMATOES, SLICED HORIZONTALLY INTO 1/2-INCH WEDGES

1 (2.8 OUNCE) CAN FRENCH-FRIED ONIONS

Combine shallots, 2 onion quarters, ginger, and garlic in a food processor; pulse into a paste.

Heat oil in a large pot over medium-high heat; cook and stir cloves, nutmeg, and cinnamon until fragrant, about 30 seconds. Add shallot paste and fry until fragrant and slightly browned, 2 to 3 minutes. Add oxtails; stir until completely covered with spices and paste and browned, about 5 minutes.

Stir remaining onion quarters, 2 carrots, and celery into the pot. Pour in enough water to cover by 2 inches. Bring to a boil; reduce heat, cover, and simmer until oxtail is tender, about 5 hours.

Stir salt, black pepper, potatoes, and 3 carrots into the pot. Increase heat and simmer soup until potatoes and carrots are tender, about 15 minutes. Add sugar and fish sauce; stir well to combine.

Ladle soup into large serving bowls and top with tomato wedges and French-fried onions.

Entree

Indonesian Satay

INGREDIENTS

3 TABLESPOONS SOY SAUCE
3 TABLESPOONS TOMATO SAUCE
1 TABLESPOON PEANUT OIL
2 CLOVES GARLIC, PEELED AND MINCED
1 PINCH GROUND BLACK PEPPER
1 PINCH GROUND CUMIN
6 SKINLESS, BONELESS CHICKEN BREAST HALVES - CUBED
1 TABLESPOON VEGETABLE OIL
1/4 CUP MINCED ONION
1 CLOVE GARLIC, PEELED AND MINCED
1 CUP WATER
1/2 CUP CHUNKY PEANUT BUTTER
2 TABLESPOONS SOY SAUCE
2 TABLESPOONS WHITE SUGAR
1 TABLESPOON LEMON JUICE
SKEWERS

In a bowl, mix soy sauce, tomato sauce, peanut oil, garlic, black pepper, and cumin. Place chicken into the mixture, and stir to coat. Cover, and marinate in the refrigerator for at least 15 minutes, but not overnight. This will make the meat too dark.

Preheat the grill for high heat.

Heat vegetable oil in a saucepan over medium heat, and sauté onion and garlic until lightly browned. Mix in water, peanut butter, soy sauce, and sugar. Cook and stir until well blended. Remove from heat, mix in lemon juice, and set aside.

Lightly oil the grill grate. Thread chicken onto skewers, and discard marinade. Grill skewers about 5 minutes per side, until chicken juices run clear. Serve with the peanut sauce.

Dessert

Banana Fritters

INGREDIENTS

1 1/4 CUPS ALL-PURPOSE FLOUR

2 TABLESPOONS GRANULATED SUGAR

1/4 TABLESPOON VANILLA POWDER

1/2 CUP MILK

1 EGG

2 TABLESPOONS BUTTER, MELTED

1 TEASPOON RUM FLAVORING

4 RIPE BANANAS, SLICED

2 CUPS OIL FOR FRYING

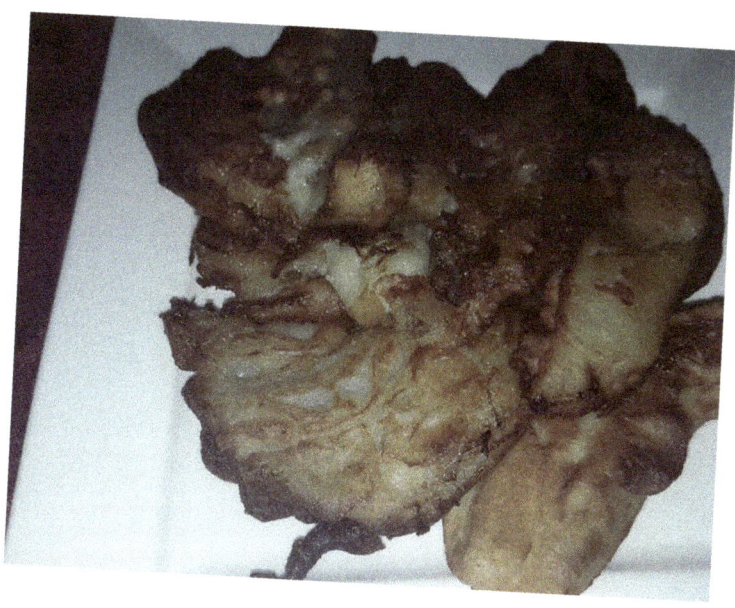

In a large bowl, combine flour, sugar and vanilla powder. Make a well in the center, and pour in milk, egg, melted butter and rum flavoring. Mix until smooth. Fold in banana slices until evenly coated.

Heat oil in a wok or deep-fryer to 375 degrees F (190 degrees C).

Drop banana mixture by tablespoon into hot oil. Fry until golden brown and crispy, 10 to 15 minutes. Remove bananas from oil, and drain on paper towels. Serve hot.

IRELAND

THE EMERALD ISLE

Dedra's Notes

Ireland is very special to me, as some of my ancestors have been from there. It was a lifelong dream of mine to go there and visit the land of my heritage, and since then, I have been again. Twice is definitely not enough, so I'm sure at some point, I'll visit the stunning Emerald Isle for a third time and many times to come! The people of Ireland are friendly, funny, and so down to Earth! They will always treat you like family, and you'll never feel a lack of company, as any random person is likely to start up a conversation! The food is down home wholesome and hearty food, and the ingredients are not expensive at all. Enjoy!

Menu

Starter

Irish Soda Bread

Entree

Chicken and Dumplings

– or –

Irish Stew

Dessert

Irish Coffee Cake

Starter

Irish Soda Bread

INGREDIENTS

4 CUPS ALL-PURPOSE FLOUR
4 TABLESPOONS WHITE SUGAR
1 TEASPOON BAKING SODA
1 TABLESPOON BAKING POWDER
1/2 TEASPOON SALT
1/2 CUP MARGARINE, SOFTENED
1 CUP BUTTERMILK
1 EGG
1/4 CUP BUTTER, MELTED
1/4 CUP BUTTERMILK

Preheat oven to 375 degrees F (190 degrees C). Lightly grease a large baking sheet.

In a large bowl, mix together flour, sugar, baking soda, baking powder, salt and margarine. Stir in 1 cup of buttermilk and egg. (If you are like me and in a place where you can't find buttermilk, try mixing a teaspoon of lemon juice into a cup of milk and leaving it to sit for 5 min.) Turn dough out onto a lightly floured surface and knead slightly. Form dough into a ball and place on prepared baking sheet. In a small bowl, combine melted butter with 1/4 cup buttermilk; brush loaf with this mixture. Use a sharp knife to cut an 'X' into the top of the loaf. This is to let the heat in evenly.

Bake in preheated oven until a toothpick inserted into the center of the loaf comes out clean, 45 to 50 minutes. Check for doneness after 30 minutes. You may continue to brush the loaf with the butter mixture while it bakes.

Entree

Chicken and Dumplings

INGREDIENTS

2 (10.75 OUNCE) CANS CONDENSED CREAM OF CHICKEN SOUP (IF YOU CAN'T FIND A CAN OF CHICKEN SOUP, TRY PREPARING IT FROM THE POWDER POUCHES)
3 CUPS WATER
1 CUP CHOPPED CELERY
2 ONIONS, QUARTERED
1 TEASPOON SALT
1/2 TEASPOON POULTRY SEASONING
1/2 TEASPOON GROUND BLACK PEPPER
4 SKINLESS, BONELESS CHICKEN BREAST HALVES
5 CARROTS, SLICED
1 (10 OUNCE) PACKAGE FROZEN GREEN PEAS
4 POTATOES, QUARTERED
3 CUPS BAKING MIX
1 1/3 CUPS MILK

In large, heavy pot, combine soup, water, chicken, celery, onion, salt, poultry seasoning, and pepper. Cover and cook over low heat about 1 1/2 hours.

Add potatoes and carrots; cover and cook another 30 minutes.

Remove chicken from pot, shred it, and return to pot. Add peas and cook only 5 minutes longer.

Add dumplings. To make dumplings: Mix baking mix and milk until a soft dough forms. Drop by tablespoonful onto bubbling stew. Simmer covered for 10 minutes, then uncover and simmer an additional 10 minutes.

Entree

Irish Stew

INGREDIENTS

1 1/2 POUNDS THICKLY SLICED BEEF BACON, DICED
6 POUNDS BONELESS LAMB SHOULDER, CUT INTO 2 INCH PIECES
1/2 TEASPOON SALT
1/2 TEASPOON GROUND BLACK PEPPER
1/2 CUP ALL-PURPOSE FLOUR
3 CLOVES GARLIC, MINCED
1 LARGE ONION, CHOPPED
1/2 CUP WATER
4 CUPS VEGETABLE STOCK
2 TEASPOONS WHITE SUGAR
4 CUPS DICED CARROTS
2 LARGE ONIONS, CUT INTO BITE-SIZE PIECES
3 POTATOES
1 TEASPOON DRIED THYME
2 BAY LEAVES
SPRIGS OF SPRING ONION
½ CUP WHITE GRAPE VINEGAR
2 TABLESPOONS OF WORCESTERSHIRE SAUCE
1 TEASPOON OF OLIVE OIL

Place beef bacon in a large, deep skillet. Cook over medium high heat until evenly brown. Drain, crumble, and set aside.

Put lamb, salt, pepper, and flour in large mixing bowl. Toss to coat meat evenly. Brown meat in frying pan with bacon fat. Add a touch of olive oil if you need additional oil.

Place meat into stock pot (leave 1/4 cup of fat in frying pan). Add the garlic and yellow onion and sauté till onion begins to become golden. Deglaze frying pan with 1/2 cup water and add the garlic-onion mixture to the stock pot with bacon pieces, vegetable stock, and sugar. Cover and simmer for 1 1/2 hours.

Add carrots, onions, potatoes, thyme, bay leaves, and vinegar to pot. Reduce heat, and simmer covered for 20 minutes until vegetables are tender.

Dessert

Irish Coffee Cake

INGREDIENTS

CAKE
175G/6OZ BUTTER OR MARGARINE
175G/6OZ SUGAR
1 LEVEL TEASPOON BAKING POWDER
2 TABLESPOONS INSTANT COFFEE DISSOLVED IN 2 TABLESPOONS HOT WATER
3 EGGS
175G/6OZ OF SELF RAISING FLOUR

SYRUP
150ML/ ¼PT STRONG BLACK COFFEE
125G/4OZ CASTER SUGAR
1 TSP. OF VANILLA EXTRACT

TOPPING
170ML CARTON CREAM
1 TSP VANILLA EXTRACT
CHOCOLATE (GRATED) OR FLAKE BAR (CRUSHED)

Preheat oven to 180°C / 350°F/Gas 4. Grease and baseline a 20cms / 8" deep cake tin.

Put all ingredients for the cake into a large mixing bowl and beat until mixture is smooth.

Transfer to the prepared tin and bake for about 40 minutes until risen and when gently pressed the cake springs back.

Remove from tin and leave on a wire tray to cool. Wash and dry cake tin.

Dissolve the sugar slowly in the coffee, boil for one minute. Then remove from heat and stir in the vanilla.

When cake is cold return cake to the clean tin, pour coffee syrup over the cake and allow to stand for a few hours.

Whip the cream and stir in the vanilla, remove the cake from the tin and cover with the whipped cream.

Chill in the fridge. Decorate with grated chocolate or crushed Flake bar. My favorite is Cadbury Flake! Yum!

ITALY

Dedra's Notes

Italy...what can I say except, "Bellissimo!" Indeed, Italy is beautiful in every way. There's a calmness in Italy, despite it being such a popular tourist destination. The locals are relaxed and appear to be content. Perhaps it's due to the fact that romance, great food and enjoyment are such integral parts of their society? Yes, Italians are all about pleasure, and that starts of course, with their amazing cuisine.

If you want to make an Italian laugh when you visit Rome next time, ask him where's the Pizza Hut or the Starbucks. Italians take great pride in their pizza, their pasta dishes, and their coffee that is to die for. Their food is ideal for a large family that likes to bond over a good meal, and then take a nice nap. I threw a coin into the Trevi Fountain while I was there, as it's said to do so is to insure that you'll visit Italy again one day. I, for one, hope that legend holds true.

Menu

Starter

Bruschetta

Entree

Italian Lamb Stew
– or –
Cacio E Pepe Spaghetti

Dessert

Chocolate Biscotti

Starter

Bruschetta

INGREDIENTS

1 FRENCH BAGUETTE, CUT INTO 1/2-INCH-THICK CIRCLES
8 PLUM TOMATOES, DICED
1 CUP CHOPPED FRESH BASIL
½ ONION, MINCED
FRESH GROUND BLACK PEPPER
2 GARLIC CLOVES

Preheat oven to 400 degrees F (200 degrees C).

Combine tomato, basil, and red onion in a small mixing bowl; stir well. Season with freshly ground black pepper. Set aside.

Arrange bread on a baking sheet. Place in oven, and bake until well toasted, approximately 5 minutes.

Remove bread from oven, and transfer to a large serving platter. Let bread cool 3 to 5 minutes.

Rub garlic into the top of each slice of toast; the toast should glisten with the garlic. Spoon the tomato mixture generously onto each slice, and serve.

95 MINUTES
6 SERVINGS

Lamb Stew

INGREDIENTS

2 TABLESPOONS OLIVE OIL
1 ½ POUNDS BONELESS LAMB SHOULDER, CUT INTO 1-INCH CUBES
SALT AND GROUND BLACK PEPPER TO TASTE
5 CLOVES OF GARLIC, SLICED THIN
½ CUP WHITE GRAPE JUICE
½ CUP CHICKEN BROTH OR VEGETABLE BROTH
4 CUPS PEELED, CHOPPED TOMATOES
1 TEASPOON DRIED OREGANO
1 BAY LEAF
4 POTATOES, PEELED AND CUT INTO 1-INCH PIECES
2 CUPS FRESH GREEN BEANS, TRIMMED
1 RED BELL PEPPER, SEEDED AND CUT INTO 1-INCH PIECES
2 SMALL ZUCCHINIS, SLICED
3 TABLESPOONS CHOPPED FRESH PARSLEY

Heat the olive oil in a Dutch oven or large, heavy-bottomed pot. Season the lamb with salt and pepper; cook in the hot oil until browned, 2 to 3 minutes. Add the garlic; cook and stir 1 minute.

Pour the grape juice and broth into the pan and bring to a boil while scraping the browned bits of food off of the bottom of the pot with a wooden spoon.

Reduce the heat to medium-low; add the tomatoes, oregano, and bay leaf to the pot.

Simmer gently until the lamb is tender, about 45 minutes.

Raise heat to medium-high. Add the potatoes, green beans, red pepper, and zucchini to the pot.

Cook until the vegetables are tender, another 15 to 20 minutes. Sprinkle the parsley over the soup. Remove the bay leaf and season with salt and pepper before serving.

Entree

Cacio E Pepe Spaghetti

INGREDIENTS

SALT

8 OZ. SPAGHETTI PASTA

4 TBSP. UNSALTED BUTTER, CUBED, DIVIDED

1 AND 1/2 TSP. FRESHLY CRACKED BLACK PEPPER

1 CUP FINELY GRATED GRANA PADANO OR

PARMESAN

1/3 CUP FINELY GRATED MOZZARELLA

½ CUP MUSHROOMS, SLICED

Bring 3 quarts of water to a boil in a 5-qt. pot. Season with salt; add pasta and cook, stirring occasionally, until about 2 minutes before tender. Drain, reserving 3/4 cup pasta cooking water.

Meanwhile, melt 2 Tbsp. butter in a large heavy skillet over medium heat. Add pepper and cook, swirling pan, until toasted, about 1 minute.

Add 1/2 cup reserved pasta water to skillet and bring to a simmer. Add pasta and remaining butter. Reduce heat to low or medium and add Grana Padano, stirring and tossing with tongs until melted. Remove pan from heat; add the Mozzarella and the mushrooms, stirring and tossing until cheese melts, sauce coats the pasta, and pasta is al dente. (You can keep on adding pasta water if sauce seems dry.) Transfer pasta to warm bowls and serve.

Dessert

Chocolate Biscotti

INGREDIENTS

1/2 CUP BUTTER, SOFTENED

2/3 CUP WHITE SUGAR

1/4 CUP UNSWEETENED COCOA POWDER

2 TEASPOONS BAKING POWDER

2 EGGS

1 ¾ CUPS ALL-PURPOSE FLOUR

4 (1 OZ.) SQUARES WHITE CHOCOLATE, CHOPPED

¾ CUP SEMISWEET CHOCOLATE CHIPS

In a large mixing bowl, cream butter and sugar with an electric mixer until light and fluffy. Gradually beat in cocoa and baking powder. Beat for 2 minutes. Beat in the eggs one at a time. Stir in flour by hand. Mix in white chocolate and chocolate chips. Cover dough, and chill for about 10 minutes.

Preheat oven to 375 degrees F (190 degrees C). Divide dough into two parts, and roll each part into a 9-inch-long log. Place logs on lightly greased cookie sheet, about 4 inches apart. Flatten slightly.

Bake for 20 to 25 minutes, or until toothpick inserted in center comes out clean. Cool on cookie sheet for 5 minutes, then carefully transfer to a wire rack to cool for one hour.

Cut each loaf into 1/2-inch-wide diagonal slices. Place slices on an ungreased cookie sheet, and bake at 325 degrees F (165 degrees C) for 9 minutes. Turn cookies over, and bake for 7 to 9 minutes. Cool completely, then store in an airtight container.

KENYA

THE LAND OF UNPARALLELED BEAUTY

Sadly, I've never been to Kenya, but it's on my list. I can say this, however. I've never met a Kenyan citizen that I didn't like, and they are always welcoming, with amazing smiles and a generosity that I'm in awe of. Their clothing is as colorful and bright as their amazing spirits and their never ending sense of humor. I guess it's no wonder that their cuisine is hearty and satisfying, food that makes you feel "well fed" indeed. Enjoy it with your family and invite a friend to feast with you.

Menu

Starter

Sukuma Wiki

Entree

Roasted Chicken with Garlic and Vegetables

– or –

Githeri

Dessert

Kenyan Sponge Cake

Starter

Sukuma Wiki

INGREDIENTS

1 POUND KALE
2 MEDIUM TOMATOES, ABOUT 1/2 POUND
1 LARGE WHITE ONION, ABOUT 1 POUND
1 TABLESPOON PEANUT OIL
1 TEASPOON CUMIN
1/2 TEASPOON CORIANDER
1/2 TEASPOON TURMERIC
1 1/2 TEASPOONS KOSHER SALT
FRESHLY GROUND BLACK PEPPER
1 LEMON, JUICED, ABOUT 3 TABLESPOONS

Chop the kale into rough 1-inch pieces, including the ribs. Roughly chop the tomatoes. (If desired, reserve about 1/4 cup fresh tomato pieces for garnish.) Peel and dice the onion.

Heat the oil in a large, deep pot, or a large wok. When it is hot, add the onion and cook for about 8 minutes over medium-high heat, stirring frequently. When the onion is getting soft, stir in the cumin, coriander, and turmeric. Stir in the tomatoes and cook for about 2 minutes.

Add the greens one handful at a time, stirring constantly to coat them with the onions, oil, and spices. When they have all been added, sprinkle the salt and a generous amount of fresh pepper over them and stir.

Pour in 1 cup water. Cover the pot and turn the heat down to medium. Cook for 10 to 20 minutes, or until the greens are tender to your taste. (I like mine fairly toothsome, so I only cook them for about 10 minutes.)

Remove the lid, turn off the heat, and toss the greens with the lemon juice. Serve hot, garnished with extra tomato, if desired.

Entree

Roasted Chicken with Garlic and Vegetables

INGREDIENTS

1 WHOLE CHICKEN
6-8 CLOVES OF GARLIC, MINCED
4 TABLESPOONS OF UNSALTED BUTTER
1 LEMON HALVED
3 SPRIGS FRESH ROSEMARY

VEGETABLES:
2 LARGE SWEET POTATOES PEELED AND CUT INTO CHUNKS
2 CARROTS, PEELED AND CUT INTO CHUNKS
3 MEDIUM SHALLOTS — HALVED OR QUARTERED
2 INCHES FRESH GINGER — PEELED AND CUT INTO SMALL PIECES
FRESH THYME FOR THE VEGETABLES
2 TABLESPOONS OLIVE OIL
SALT AND PEPPER TO TASTE

Start by first preparing the chicken. Remove the giblets, trim any excess fat from around the bird's cavity then rinse and dry it thoroughly. The drier the chicken, the crispier it will be.

Tie the legs together with a kitchen twine and place the bird in a baking dish or a roasting pan.

Let the chicken sit at room temperature uncovered for one hour before roasting.

Prepare the vegetables in a large bowl and drizzling with olive oil, season with salt, pepper and thyme. Toss to combine and set aside.

Preheat oven to 220 degrees Celsius

Generously season chicken broth inside and out with salt and pepper

Melt butter in a pan over medium heat and add the minced garlic, fry till the garlic is soft. Brush the melted garlic-butter all over the bird including the cavity. Place the two halved lemons and the rosemary sprigs inside the cavity. Place the prepared vegetables around the chicken.

Roast the chicken for one hour basting it between using a spoon and tilting the pan to collect some juice and spooning it on top of the chicken.

Once done, remove the chicken from the roasting pan and transfer it to a cutting board to serving platter. Let it rest for 10 minutes before carving.

Serve with accompanying vegetables and enjoy!

Entree

Githeri

INGREDIENTS

2 CUPS OR 3-4 EARS OF CORN, CUT FRESH OFF THE COB
OR FROZEN
GREEN PEAS
GREEN BEANS
A BIT OF KALE
2 CUPS OF COOKED BEANS (ANY TYPE)
WATER TO COVER
BUTTER
1 TEASPOON OF CORIANDER
A PINCH OF CHILI POWDER
SALT AND PEPPER TO TASTE

Note that this dish normally doesn't contain green beans, kale, or green peas, but I added them because they are delicious in this dish!

Melt butter in a large pot.

Add the corn, beans, kale and green beans to the pot and add the coriander and the pinch of Chili powder.

Stir fry for 2 minutes.

Add enough water just to cover.

Season with salt and pepper and bring to a boil over medium heat.

Reduce heat to low and simmer until cooked through, 8 to 10 minutes.

Serve.

Dessert

Kenyan Sponge Cake

INGREDIENTS

1 CUP FLOUR
¾ CUP SUGAR
4 EGGS, AT ROOM TEMPERATURE
1 TEASPOON GROUND CARDAMOM POWDER
4-6 CARDAMOM PODS, OPENED (ONLY USE THE SEEDS)
A PINCH OF CINNAMON POWDER

EXTRAS:
1 TABLESPOON FLOUR AND BUTTER (FOR DUSTING)

Preheat to 180 degrees.

Add eggs and sugar into a mixing bowl and mix using an electric whisk or a hand mixture until thick and voluminous

In a separate bowl, mix the rest mix the rest of the dry ingredients and sift in gently into the egg and sugar mixture. Use a spatula to fold in the flour until there are no more lumps in the floor.

Prepare a baking pan by lightly greasing it with butter and dusting it with flour then pour the cake mixture into it.

Place it in the oven until golden brown. Keep it in for around 30-35 minutes or until a toothpick comes out clean when you prod into the cake.

Cool completely on a wire rack before serving.

KOREA

THE LAND OF THE MORNING CALM

Korea is an up and coming country in so many ways. They are breaking ground in films, in music, and they seem to really enjoy western culture and infl uence; however, there's a growing concern that the "traditional" ways are dwindling, including the food, which is a great tragedy, as traditional Korean food is not only fl avorful, but beautiful, as it's considered very important to deliver each dish with proper presentation. An old Korean proverb maintains, "If it looks good, it tastes good."

Menu

Starter

Korean Crab Cakes

Entree

Maple Syrup Korean Teriyaki Chicken
– or –
Jap Chae Korean Glass Noodles

Dessert

Manju (Korean Sweet Bread)

Starter

Korean Crab Cakes

INGREDIENTS

¼ CUP MAYONNAISE

2 TABLESPOONS CHOPPED FRESH CILANTRO

1 TABLESPOON CHOPPED FRESH GINGER

2 TEASPOONS ASIAN FISH SAUCE (NUOC MAM OR NAM PLA)

1 (6 OUNCE) CAN CRABMEAT – DRAINED, FLAKED AND CARTILAGE REMOVED

3 OUNCES CHOPPED SHRIMP

1 ½ CUPS FRESH BREADCRUMBS, MADE FROM CRUSTLESS FRENCH BREAD

SALT AND PEPPER TO TASTE

1 ½ TABLESPOONS PEANUT OIL

In a medium bowl, mix together mayonnaise, cilantro, fresh ginger, and fish sauce. Mix in crab, shrimp, and 1/2 cup bread crumbs. Season with salt and pepper to taste.

Place remaining 1 cup breadcrumbs on a plate or shallow bowl. Drop 1/4 of the crab mixture onto breadcrumbs, and turn to coat. Shape into a circle or oval. repeat with remaining crab mixture.

Heat oil in a heavy skillet over medium heat. Cook cakes in oil for about 5 minutes per side, or until golden brown and cooked through.

Entree

Maple Syrup Korean Teriyaki Chicken

INGREDIENTS

1 CUP WATER

1/3 CUP MAPLE SYRUP

3 TABLESPOONS DARK SESAME OIL

2 CLOVES GARLIC, CRUSHED

1 TABLESPOON MINCED FRESH GINGER ROOT

2 TEASPOONS GROUND BLACK PEPPER

5 SKINLESS, BONELESS CHICKEN BREAST HALVES

1 CUP BROWN RICE

2 CUPS WATER

2 TABLESPOONS CORNSTARCH

Mix the soy sauce, 1 cup water, maple syrup, sesame oil, garlic, ginger, and pepper in a large resealable plastic bag. Set aside 1/3 cup of the mixture. Place the chicken in the bag, seal, and marinate at least 2 hours in the refrigerator. That's the easy part.

Place the rice in a saucepan with 2 cups water, and bring to a boil. Cover, reduce heat to low, and simmer 45 minutes.

Preheat the oven broiler. Lightly grease a baking dish.

Pour marinade from the bag into a saucepan, and bring to a boil. Mix in the cornstarch, and cook and stir until thickened.

Place chicken in the prepared baking dish. Basting frequently with the reserved 1/3 cup marinade, broil 8 minutes per side, until juices run clear. Place chicken over the cooked rice, and top with boiled marinade to serve.

Entree

Korean Glass Noodles

INGREDIENTS

1 TEASPOON SESAME OIL

2 TABLESPOONS WHITE SUGAR

1 TABLESPOON VEGETABLE OIL

2 CLOVES GARLIC, MINCED

¾ CUP THINLY SLICED ONIONS

2 CARROTS, CUT INTO MATCHSTICK SIZE PIECES

½ POUND ASPARAGUS, THINLY SLICED

3 GREEN ONIONS CUT INTO 1-INCH PIECES

½ CUP DRIED SHIITAKE MUSHROOMS, SOAKED UNTIL SOFT, THEN SLICED INTO STRIPS

1 TABLESPOON SESAME SEEDS

1 ½ TEASPOONS SESAME OIL

Fill a large pot with lightly salted water and bring to a rolling boil over high heat.

Once the water is boiling, stir in the dang myun noodles, and return to a boil. Cook the noodles uncovered, stirring occasionally, until the noodles have cooked through, but are still firm to the bite, 4 to 5 minutes.

Rinse with cold water and drain well in a colander set in the sink. Toss noodles with 1 teaspoon of sesame oil. Set aside. Whisk soy sauce and sugar in a small bowl. Set aside.

Heat the vegetable oil in a skillet over medium-high heat. Stir in the garlic, onion, carrots, and asparagus; cook and stir until the vegetables have softened, about 5 minutes.

Stir in green onions and shiitake mushrooms and continue cooking and stirring for 30 seconds. Pour in the soy sauce mixture, then add the noodles. Cook and stir until the noodles are warmed through, 2 to 3 minutes. Remove from heat and toss with sesame seeds and the remaining 1 1/2 teaspoon of sesame oil.

Enjoy with Chopsticks if you can, because it literally makes it taste better!

Dessert

Manju

INGREDIENTS

2 CUPS WHITE SUGAR

1 CUP BUTTER, SOFTENED

4 EGGS

1 TEASPOON VANILLA EXTRACT

5 CUPS ALL-PURPOSE FLOUR

2 TABLESPOONS BAKING POWDER

1 (18 OUNCE) CAN KOSHI AN (SWEETENED RED BEAN PASTE)

1/4 CUP EVAPORATED MILK, OR AS NEEDED

Preheat oven to 375 degrees F (190 degrees C). Grease 2 baking sheets.

Beat sugar and butter with an electric mixer in a large bowl until smooth and creamy. Beat eggs, 1 at a time, into creamed butter until smooth; add vanilla extract and beat well.

Sift flour and baking powder together in a bowl. Gradually stir flour mixture into butter mixture, mixing well after each addition, until dough is smooth.

Generously flour your hands. Make walnut-size balls from the dough and press into 4-inch circles on a floured surface, making the circles thicker in the center and thinner on the edges.

Spoon about 1 1/2 teaspoons koshi an in the center of each dough circle. Gather the edges together and pinch dough around the filling until sealed. Place dough balls, pinched-side down, on the prepared baking sheets about 2 inches apart. Brush dough balls with evaporated milk.

You can get creative here if you like and draw patterns into the dough…Leaves, Circles, etc.…Or just go for the standard cookie shape.

Bake in the preheated oven until tops are lightly browned, about 15 minutes.

Lebanon

The Land of Milk and Honey

When we visited Lebanon, the first thing I noticed was the roses. Fortunately for us, we stayed in a private home on a mountain side while we were there, and each day, I remember waking up to the fresh smell of the mountain air and the wild roses. It was some of the best sleep I had ever had in my life. Wild cherries were growing all around our vacation rental, so we were able to pick them fresh and eat as many of them as we wanted. The flavor was outstanding, and all of our culinary experiences there were equally pleasurable. Fresh grilled fish, mixed grilled kabob of all varieties, paired with hummus and fresh bread made in clay ovens were to be found in each tourist site. The sweetness of the air goes into all the fruits and vegetables grown there, so if you're lucky enough to buy produce from Lebanon, don't hesitate!

Menu

Starter

Fattoush

Entree

Kofta Kebab
– or –
Bean Salad

Dessert

Namoora

Starter

Fattoush

INGREDIENTS

3 PITA BREADS, TORN INTO PIECES
OIL FOR FRYING
2 CUPS TORN ROMAINE LETTUCE
2 TOMATOES, CHOPPED
2 SMALL CUCUMBERS, PEELED AND DICED
1 GREEN BELL PEPPER, CHOPPED
3 GREEN ONIONS, MINCED
15 FRESH MINT LEAVES, CHOPPED
1/4 CUP CHOPPED FRESH PARSLEY
1 TEASPOON CILANTRO

Heat oil in a large skillet over medium-high heat. Place pita pieces into the skillet without crowding. Fry in batches until browned; then remove to paper towels. It's important that these pieces get very crispy.

Place romaine lettuce, tomatoes, cucumbers, bell pepper, green onions, mint leaves, parsley, and cilantro into a large bowl.

Pour lemon juice and white vinegar into a small bowl. Season with salt, lemon pepper, onion flakes, celery salt, and garlic powder. Stir in olive oil.

Gently toss salad with fried pita pieces and dressing. Adjust seasonings to taste, and serve. Easy and so delicious and fresh tasting!

DRESSING

1/4 CUP LEMON JUICE
2 TEASPOONS WHITE VINEGAR
1 PINCH SALT
1/2 TEASPOON LEMON PEPPER
1/2 TEASPOON DRIED ONION FLAKES
1 PINCH CELERY SALT
1 PINCH GARLIC POWDER
1/4 CUP OLIVE OIL

Entree

Kofta Kebab

INGREDIENTS

1 TEASPOON SESAME OIL

2 TABLESPOONS WHITE SUGAR

1 TABLESPOON VEGETABLE OIL

2 CLOVES GARLIC, MINCED

¾ CUP THINLY SLICED ONIONS

2 CARROTS, CUT INTO MATCHSTICK SIZE PIECES

½ POUND ASPARAGUS, THINLY SLICED

3 GREEN ONIONS CUT INTO 1-INCH PIECES

½ CUP DRIED SHIITAKE MUSHROOMS, SOAKED UNTIL SOFT, THEN SLICED INTO STRIPS

1 TABLESPOON SESAME SEEDS

1 ½ TEASPOONS SESAME OIL

Mash the garlic into a paste with the salt using a mortar and pestle or the flat side of a chef's knife on your cutting board. Crush the garlic so as to release the flavor very well in the meat.

Mix the garlic into the lamb along with the onion, parsley, coriander, cumin, cinnamon, allspice, cayenne pepper, ginger, and pepper in a mixing bowl until well blended. Form the mixture into 28 balls. Form each ball around the tip of a skewer, flattening into a 2 inch oval; repeat with the remaining skewers. Place the kebabs onto a baking sheet, cover, and refrigerate at least 30 minutes, or up to 12 hours.

Preheat an outdoor grill for medium heat, and lightly oil grate.

Cook the skewers on the preheated grill, turning occasionally, until the lamb has cooked to your desired degree of doneness, about 6 minutes for medium.

Entree

Bean Salad

INGREDIENTS

1 1/2 CUPS DRIED BLACK-EYED PEAS, SOAKED OVERNIGHT
1/3 CUP CHOPPED CELERY, WITH LEAVES
1 1/2 CUPS SHREDDED CARROT
3/4 CUP CHOPPED FRESH PARSLEY
1/2 CUP CHOPPED WHITE ONION
1/8 CUP CHOPPED FRESH MINT

DRESSING:
1/4 CUP OLIVE OIL
2 ORANGES, JUICED
1/2 LEMON, JUICED
1 GARLIC CLOVE, PRESSED
1/2 TEASPOON GROUND CORIANDER
1/2 TEASPOON SALT
1/8 TEASPOON FRESHLY GROUND BLACK PEPPER
1 TEASPOON BROWN SUGAR

Place the beans in a saucepan with enough water to cover them by one inch. Bring beans to a slow boil. Reduce heat to low, and simmer until tender but not mushy (about 35 minutes). Set aside to cool.

When the beans have cooled, place them in a large bowl. Add the celery, carrots, parsley, white onion, and mint; toss to blend.

For dressing, blend olive oil, orange and lemon juice, garlic, coriander, salt, pepper, and brown sugar in a blender for 6 seconds. Transfer to a small saucepan, and simmer over low heat for five minutes. Remove from heat, and cool. Pour dressing over the bean salad, and refrigerate for at least 1 hour before serving. This dish is brilliant as a snack, eaten with Pita Bread or as a main course over rice.

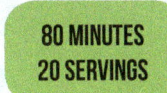
Dessert

Namoora

INGREDIENTS

1 TABLESPOON TAHINI (SESAME SEED PASTE)

2 CUPS DRY CREAM OF WHEAT CEREAL

1 1/2 CUPS WHITE SUGAR

2 TEASPOONS BAKING POWDER

1 CUP PLAIN YOGURT

1 TABLESPOON BUTTER, SOFTENED

16 BLANCHED ALMOND HALVES

2 CUPS WHITE SUGAR

2 CUPS WATER

1 TEASPOON LEMON JUICE

1 TABLESPOON BUTTER

1 TEASPOON ORANGE FLOWER WATER (OPTIONAL)

Line a 9x13-inch glass baking dish with aluminum foil and generously butter the foil. Spread the tahini evenly over the bottom of the prepared pan in a thin layer.

Mix together farina cereal with 1 1/2 cup of sugar and baking powder in a bowl. Mix in the yogurt and 1 tablespoon of softened butter gently with your hands until the dough is smooth. Spread dough out into the prepared baking dish. Pat the surface smooth. Cover the dish with foil, and allow to stand at room temperature for 2 hours. With a sharp knife, cut the dough into

16 squares; push an almond half gently into the top of each square.

Preheat oven to 400 degrees F (200 degrees C).

Bake in the preheated oven until the dessert is set and the top is lightly golden brown, about 30 minutes.

While the dessert is baking, make the syrup. Place 2 cups of sugar into a saucepan with the water, and bring to a boil over medium heat, stirring constantly to dissolve sugar. Stir in the lemon juice, and boil the syrup for 5 minutes; stir in butter and orange flower water until combined. Pour the hot syrup over the dessert as soon as it comes out of the oven. Let cool for 1 to 2 hours to let the syrup absorb before serving. This is so good with a cup of hot black coffee!

Mexico

Dedra's Notes

Being American, and living in a Southern State like Alabama, I always thought I'd travel to Mexico one day. Of all the countries that Americans usually choose to travel to, Mexico is number one on that list because it's close, it's economical, and its fun! The food has also come into American culture more than any other type of cuisine. Even in a highly Southern location

like Alabama, I grew up having tacos, burritos and quesadillas as viable options for lunch and dinner. Mexican food is fun, colorful, and spicy—very reflective of its origin, and these dishes are always household favorites!

Menu

Starter

Guacamole

Entree

Tacos De Matamoros

– or –

Black Bean Burritos

Dessert

Mexican Wedding Cookies

Starter

Guacamole

INGREDIENTS

3 AVOCADOS — PEELED, PITTED, AND MASHED

1 LIME, JUICED

1 TEASPOON SALT

½ CUP DICED ONION

3 TABLESPOONS CHOPPED FRESH CILANTRO

2 PLUM TOMATOES, DICED

1 TEASPOON MINCED GARLIC

1 PINCH CAYENNE PEPPER (OPTIONAL)

In a medium bowl, mash together the avocados, lime juice, and salt. Mix in onion, cilantro, tomatoes, and garlic. Stir in cayenne pepper. Refrigerate 1 hour for best flavor, or serve immediately. Easy!

Entree

Tacos De Matamoros

INGREDIENTS

2 POUNDS GROUND CHUCK
2 TABLESPOONS CHILI POWDER
2 TABLESPOONS PAPRIKA
1 ½ TEASPOONS CUMIN
1 TEASPOON SALT
½ TEASPOONS GARLIC POWDER
2 CLOVES GARLIC, CHOPPED
½ MEDIUM GREEN BELL PEPPER, CHOPPED
½ MEDIUM ONION, CHOPPED
12 (6 INCH) CORN TORTILLAS
12 OUNCES QUESO ASADERO (WHITE MEXICAN CHEESE, BUT IF YOU CAN'T FIND THIS, A MIXED VARIETY OF GRATED CHEDDAR AND MOZZARELLA WILL DO)
1 (8 OUNCE) CONTAINER SOUR CREAM
1 LARGE TOMATO, DICED
2 CUPS SHREDDED LETTUCE

Place the ground chuck in a large skillet, and season with chili powder, paprika, cumin, salt, garlic powder, and garlic. Pour in enough water to cover. Bring to a boil. Reduce heat to low, and simmer 1 hour. Add more water as necessary during cook time, and break the meat into small pieces.

Mix the bell pepper and onion into the skillet, and continue to simmer 30 minutes. Drain and reserve juices. Skim the fat from the juices. Mix 5 tablespoons of the remaining juices back into the skillet with the beef, and cook until heated through.

Serve the beef on the tortillas. Garnish with queso asadero, sour cream, tomato, and lettuce.

Entree

Black Bean Burritos

INGREDIENTS

2 (10 INCH) FLOUR TORTILLAS

2 TABLESPOONS VEGETABLE OIL

1 SMALL ONION, CHOPPED

½ RED BELL PEPPER, CHOPPED

1 TEASPOON MINCED GARLIC

1 (15 OUNCE) CAN BLACK BEANS, RINSED AND DRAINED

1 TEASPOON MINCED JALAPENO PEPPERS

3 OUNCES SOY CHEESE

½ TEASPOON SALT

2 TABLESPOONS CHOPPED FRESH CILANTRO

Wrap vegan (just check the ingredients on the packaging for animal origin) tortillas in foil and place in oven heated to 350 degrees F (175 degrees C). Bake for 15 minutes or until heated through.

Heat oil in a 10-inch skillet over medium heat. Place onion, bell pepper, garlic and jalapenos in skillet, cook for 2 minutes stirring occasionally. Pour beans into skillet, cook 3 minutes stirring.

Cut vegan soy cheese into cubes and add to skillet with salt. Cook for 2 minutes stirring occasionally. Stir cilantro into mixture.

Spoon mixture evenly down center of warmed tortilla and roll tortillas up. Serve immediately.

Dessert

Mexican Wedding Cookies

INGREDIENTS

1 CUP BUTTER

1/2 CUP WHITE SUGAR

2 TEASPOONS VANILLA EXTRACT

2 TEASPOONS WATER

2 CUPS ALL-PURPOSE FLOUR

1 CUP CHOPPED ALMONDS

1/2 CUP CONFECTIONERS' SUGAR

In a medium bowl, cream the butter and sugar. Stir in vanilla and water. Add the flour and almonds, mix until blended. Cover and chill for 3 hours.

Preheat oven to 325 degrees.

Shape dough into balls or crescents. Place on an unprepared cookie sheet and bake for 15 to 20 minutes in the preheated oven. Remove from pan to cool on wire racks. When cookies are cool, roll in confectioners' sugar. Store at room temperature in an airtight container. I know these are an unusual choice, but believe me, after a heavy Mexican meal, they are great with a steaming cup of coffee!

Morocco

LAND OF ANCIENT MAGIC

Morocco is a meeting place for not only Arabic culture, but French and other African countries as well. The people are as colorful as their art and architecture, and have a history of folklore, music, magic and tradition that's straight out of the pages of fairy tales. Their food is rich in spices and bursting with a unique mix of sweet and savory fl avors.

Menu

Starter

Moroccan Lentil Soup

Entree

Moroccan Tagine
– or –
Make–Ahead Vegan Moroccan Stew

Dessert

Sfinge

Starter

Moroccan Lentil Soup

INGREDIENTS

2 ONIONS, CHOPPED
2 CLOVES GARLIC, MINCED
1 TEASPOON GRATED FRESH GINGER
6 CUPS WATER
1 CUP RED LENTILS
1 (15 OUNCE) CAN GARBANZO BEANS, DRAINED
1 (19 OUNCE) CAN CANNELLINI BEANS
1 (14.5 OUNCE) CAN DICED TOMATOES
½ CUP DICED CARROTS
½ CUP CHOPPED CELERY
1 TEASPOON GRAHAM MASALA
1 ½ TEASPOONS GROUND CARDAMOM
½ TEASPOON GROUND CAYENNE PEPPER
½ TEASPOON GROUND CUMIN
1 TABLESPOON OLIVE OIL

In large pot sauté; the onions, garlic, and ginger in a little olive oil for about 5 minutes.

Add the water, lentils, chickpeas, white kidney beans, diced tomatoes, carrots, celery, Graham Masala, cardamom, cayenne pepper and cumin. Bring to a boil for a few minutes then simmer for 1 to 1 1/2 hours or longer, until the lentils are soft.

Puree half the soup in a food processor or blender. Return the pureed soup to the pot, stir and enjoy!

Entree

Moroccan Tagine

INGREDIENTS

3 TABLESPOONS OLIVE OIL, DIVIDED

2 POUNDS OF LAMB MEAT, CUT INTO 1 1/2 INCH CUBES

2 TEASPOONS PAPRIKA

1/4 TEASPOON GROUND TURMERIC

1/2 TEASPOON GROUND CUMIN

1/4 TEASPOON CAYENNE PEPPER

1 TEASPOON GROUND CINNAMON

1/4 TEASPOON GROUND CLOVES

1/2 TEASPOON GROUND CARDAMOM

1 TEASPOON KOSHER SALT

1/2 TEASPOON GROUND GINGER

1 PINCH SAFFRON

3/4 TEASPOON GARLIC POWDER

3/4 TEASPOON GROUND CORIANDER

2 MEDIUM ONIONS, CUT INTO 1-INCH CUBES

5 CARROTS, PEELED, CUT INTO FOURTHS, THEN SLICED LENGTHWISE INTO THIN STRIPS

3 CLOVES GARLIC, MINCED

1 TABLESPOON FRESHLY GRATED GINGER

1 LEMON, ZESTED

1 (14.5 OUNCE) CAN HOMEMADE CHICKEN BROTH OR LOW-SODIUM CANNED BROTH

1 TABLESPOON SUN-DRIED TOMATO PASTE

1 TABLESPOON HONEY

1 TABLESPOON CORNSTARCH (OPTIONAL)

1 TABLESPOON WATER (OPTIONAL)

1 CUP GREEN BEANS

Place diced lamb in a bowl, toss with 2 tablespoons of the olive oil, and set aside. In a large resealable bag, toss together the paprika, turmeric, cumin, cayenne, cinnamon, cloves, cardamom, salt, ginger, saffron, garlic powder, and coriander; mix well.

Add the lamb to the bag, and toss around to coat well. Refrigerate at least 8 hours, or perhaps it works best to leave it overnight.

Heat 1 tablespoon of olive oil in a large, heavy bottomed pot over medium-high heat. Add 1/3 of the lamb, and brown well.

Remove to a plate, and repeat with remaining lamb.

Add onions, green beans and carrots to the pot and cook for 5 minutes.

Stir in the fresh garlic and ginger; continue cooking for an additional 5 minutes.

Return the lamb to the pot and stir in the lemon zest, chicken broth, tomato paste, and honey.

Bring to a boil, then reduce heat to low, cover, and simmer for 1 1/2 to 2 hours, stirring occasionally, until the meat is tender.

If the consistency of the tagine is too thin, you may thicken it with a mixture of cornstarch and water during the last 5 minutes.

Entree

Moroccan Vegan Stew

INGREDIENTS

SPICE MIXTURE:

1 ¼ TEASPOON GROUND CINNAMON

1 TEASPOON GROUND CUMIN

1 TEASPOON KOSHER SALT

½ TEASPOON GROUND GINGER

1/8 TEASPOON GROUND CLOVES

¼ TEASPOON GROUND NUTMEG

¼ TEASPOON GROUND TURMERIC

1/8 TEASPOON CURRY POWDER

STEW VEGETABLES:

1 TABLESPOON BUTTER

1 SWEET ONION, CHOPPED

2 CUPS FINELY SHREDDED KALE

4 (14 OUNCE) CANS ORGANIC VEGETABLE BROTH

1 (15 OUNCE) CAN GARBANZO BEANS, DRAINED

1 (14.5 OUNCE) CAN DICED TOMATOES, UNDRAINED

3 LARGE POTATOES, PEELED AND DICED

2 SWEET POTATOES, PEELED AND DICED

4 LARGE CARROTS, CHOPPED

1 CUP DRIED LENTILS, RINSED

½ CUP CHOPPED DRIED APRICOTS

1 TABLESPOON AGAVE SYRUP

1 TEASPOON GROUND BLACK PEPPER, TO TASTE

1 TABLESPOON CORNSTARCH (OPTIONAL)

Combine cinnamon, cumin, salt, ginger, cloves, nutmeg, turmeric, and curry powder in a large bowl.

Melt butter in a large pot over medium heat. Cook the onion in the butter until soft and just beginning to brown, 5 to 10 minutes. Stir in kale and spice mixture; cook until kale begins to wilt and spices are fragrant, about 2 minutes.

Pour the vegetable broth into the pot. Stir garbanzo beans, tomatoes, potatoes, sweet potatoes, carrots, lentils, apricots, and agave, into the broth; bring to boil, reduce heat to low, and simmer until vegetables and lentils are cooked and tender, about 30 minutes. Season stew with black pepper.

Dissolve cornstarch in water; stir into stew and simmer thickened, about 5 minutes.

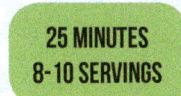

**25 MINUTES
8-10 SERVINGS**

Dessert

Sfinge

INGREDIENTS

3 CUPS FLOUR
2 TEASPOONS YEAST
1 TEASPOON SALT
1 1/4 CUP WARM WATER
2 INCHES SUNFLOWER OIL FOR FRYING
SUGAR, FOR GARNISH (OPTIONAL, BUT I THINK IT LOOKS PRETTY!)

In a small bowl, dissolve the yeast in a little warm water and set aside to proof for 10 or 15 minutes.

In a large bowl, combine the flour with the salt, then add the water and yeast mixture.

Stir vigorously with a thick wooden spoon (or your hand) until smooth. The dough should be too sticky to knead or shape, almost like a thick batter.

Cover the bowl with a towel and leave the dough to rise for three to four hours, until double or triple in bulk.

In a wide, deep pot, heat an inch or more of sunflower oil over medium heat until hot.

Get a bowl of water and set it out. Dip your hands in the water, then pull off a piece of dough about the size of a small plum. Use your fingers to make a hole in the ball of dough, stretch the hole wide to make a ring, then place the dough in the hot oil.

Repeat with additional portions of dough, until you've added as many sfenje as you can get comfortably in your pot. Wet your hands as necessary to keep the dough from sticking as you work with it.

Fry the sfenje until golden brown, turning once or twice. Remove the cooked sfenje to a plate lined with paper towels to drain.

Repeat the shaping and frying until you've used up all the dough.

If you want to, garnish the hot sfenje by dipping them in granulated sugar or by dusting with powdered sugar. I think they look more festive like that.

Serve the sfenje hot or warm. Who likes a cold donut?

Sfenje will not stay fresh very long at room temperature. It's best to freeze leftover Sfenje and then reheat in the oven when needed. Thankfully, they freeze beautifully.

PHILIPPINES

Dedra's Notes

The Philippines is the home of some of the world's best beaches, tropical tastes, and the most hard working and friendly people that you could ever meet. I've never been to the Philippines, but I've made many friends from there, and I've had the pleasure of being invited to dine with many of them. A great misconception is that Filipino food is exactly the same as Chinese or any other Asian culture, but that couldn't be farther from the truth. The tropical environment is definitely reflected in the food, as much of the cuisine is sweet, with plenty of coconut and mango, and the meats and seafood dishes are grilled or prepared in one pot. Easy and delicious!

Menu

Starter

Prawn Peanut Soup

Entree

Grilled Chicken Adobo

– or –

Filipino Spaghetti

Dessert

Mocha Chiffon Cake

Starter

Prawns in Peanut Soup

INGREDIENTS

2 CUPS WATER

SALT TO TASTE

2 1/2 POUNDS PEELED AND DEVEINED PRAWNS

3/4 POUND FRESH GREEN BEANS, TRIMMED

1 LARGE EGGPLANT, DICED

1/2 POUND BOK CHOY, CHOPPED

2 TABLESPOONS OLIVE OIL

1 ONION, CHOPPED

2 CLOVES GARLIC, MINCED

1 TEASPOON ACHIOTE POWDER (IF YOU CAN'T FIND THIS, USE ½ TEASPOON OF TURMERIC AND A ½ TEASPOON OF SWEET PAPRIKA)

3 TABLESPOONS SMOOTH PEANUT BUTTER

Bring the water and salt to a boil in a large pot. Add the prawns to the water and return to a boil; cook at a boil for 5 minutes. Remove the prawns with a strainer and set aside.

Cook the beans, eggplant, and bok choy in the water until slightly tender, about 3 minutes.

Drain and keep the liquid aside. Set the vegetables aside.

Heat the olive oil in a large skillet over medium heat; cook and stir the onion and garlic in the hot oil until fragrant, about 5 minutes.

Sprinkle the achiote powder over the mixture; stir until you produce an even orange-red color.

Add the peanut butter and continue stirring until the peanut butter has melted evenly into the mixture. Stir the reserved water into the mixture and bring to a boil; cook at a boil for 3 minutes before stirring in the prawns and vegetables.

Continue boiling together 2 minutes more before serving

Entree

Grilled Chicken Adobo

INGREDIENTS

1 ½ CUPS SOY SAUCE

1 ½ CUPS WATER

¾ CUPS VINEGAR

3 TABLESPOONS HONEY

1 ½ TABLESPOONS MINCED GARLIC

3 BAY LEAVES

½ TEASPOON BLACK PEPPER

3 POUNDS SKINLESS, BONELESS CHICKEN

Preheat an outdoor grill for high heat, and lightly oil grate.

In a large pot, mix soy sauce, water, vinegar, honey, garlic, bay leaves, and pepper. Bring the mixture to a boil, and place the chicken into the pot. Reduce heat, cover, and cook 35 to 40 minutes.

Remove chicken, drain on paper towels, and set aside. Discard bay leaves. Return the mixture to a boil, and cook until reduced to about 1 1/2 cups.

Place chicken on the prepared grill, about 5 minutes on each side, until browned and crisp. Serve with the remaining soy sauce mixture.

Entree

Filipino Spaghetti

INGREDIENTS

2 POUNDS SPAGHETTI
1 TABLESPOON VEGETABLE OIL
1 HEAD GARLIC, MINCED
1 ONION, CHOPPED
2-POUND GROUND BEEF
SALT AND PEPPER TO TASTE
1 (26.5 OUNCE) CAN SPAGHETTI SAUCE
1 (14 OUNCE) JAR BANANA KETCHUP
¼ CUP WHITE SUGAR
½ CUP WATER
1 POUND HOT DOGS, SLICED DIAGONALLY
½ CUP SHREDDED CHEDDAR CHEESE

Fill a large pot with lightly salted water and bring to a rolling boil over high heat. Once the water is boiling, stir in the spaghetti, and return to a boil. Cook the pasta uncovered, stirring occasionally, until the pasta has cooked through, but is still firm to the bite, about 12 minutes.

Drain well in a colander set in the sink.

Heat the vegetable oil in a skillet over medium heat. Stir in the garlic and onion; cook and stir until the onion has softened and turned translucent, about 5 minutes.

Stir in the beef; season with salt and pepper. Cook and stir until the meat has browned.

Pour in the spaghetti sauce, banana ketchup, sugar, and water. Simmer until the sauce has thickened, about 15 minutes. Stir in hot dog slices and continue to cook until hot dogs are heated through. Serve over spaghetti with Cheddar cheese sprinkled on top.

Dessert

Mocha Chiffon Cake

INGREDIENTS

2 1/3 CUPS ALL-PURPOSE FLOUR

1 CUP WHITE SUGAR

1 TABLESPOON BAKING POWDER

1 TEASPOON SALT

2/3 CUP BREWED COFFEE

1/2 CUP COOKING OIL

8 EGG YOLKS (SEPARATE 8 EGGS)

8 EGG WHITES

1/2 TEASPOON CREAM OF TARTAR

1/2 CUP WHITE SUGAR

Preheat an oven to 325 degrees F (165 degrees C).

Sift the flour, 1 cup sugar, baking powder, and salt together in a bowl. Make a well in the center of the flour mixture. Pour the coffee, oil, and egg yolks into the well; beat well by hand until the batter is smooth with no lumps.

Beat egg whites with the cream of tartar in a large bowl until foamy. Gradually add 1/2 cup sugar, continuing to beat until stiff peaks form. Lift your beater or whisk straight up: the egg whites should form a sharp peak that holds its shape. Fold the batter into the egg whites; pour into a non-stick fluted tube pan.

Bake in the preheated oven until a toothpick inserted into the center comes out clean, about 60 minutes. Cool in the pans for 10 minutes before removing to cool completely on a wire rack.

Loosen the sides with a knife and release the cake onto a serving platter.

POLAND

THE LAND OF A THOUSAND LAKES

Dedra's Notes

I must admit that when I always thought of Poland, I am embarrassed to admit that I always thought of a winter wasteland. Images of world war 2 occupied my thoughts, and I admit that this was very short sighted of me. I'm very happy that I included Poland on my list of countries to explore in the kitchen, as it's opened my eyes to a magical land of music and joyful souls. The cuisine is hearty and filling, as I imagine the people enjoy as they curl up next to a lovely fireplace on a starry winter night.

Menu

Starter

White Bean, Kale and Kielbasa Soup

Entree

Sweet Polish Sausage

– or –

Baked Chicken Reuben

Dessert

Chocolate Babka

Starter

White Bean, Kale and Kielbasa Soup

INGREDIENTS

1 BUNCH KALE, STEMS REMOVED AND DISCARDED

1 TABLESPOON OLIVE OIL

10 OUNCE KIELBASA BEEF SAUSAGE, SLICED THIN

1 BUNCH GREEN ONIONS, SLICED

3 CUPS CHICKEN BROTH

1 (15.5 OUNCE) CAN WHITE BEANS, DRAINED AND RINSED

½ TEASPOON SALT

1 PINCH GROUND BLACK PEPPER TO TASTE

1/8 CUP GROUND PARMESAN CHEESE, OR TO TASTE

Roll kale leaves into tight tubes and cut crosswise into 1/4-inch strips.

Heat oil in a large, heavy saucepan over medium heat.

Cook and stir beef kielbasa in hot oil until browned, about 5 minutes.

Stir green onion with sausage; cook until onions soften, about 3 minutes. Add kale; cook and stir until kale wilts, about 3 minutes.

Pour chicken broth over kielbasa mixture; add beans and stir. Bring the mixture to a boil, reduce heat to low, and cook at a simmer until kale is completely tender, about 15 minutes. Season mixture with salt and pepper and top with Parmesan cheese.

120 MINUTES
4 SERVINGS

Entree

Sweet Polish Sausage

INGREDIENTS

2 POUND BEEF OR CHICKEN KIELBASA SAUSAGE, CUT INTO 1 INCH PIECES

1/3 CUP WORCESTERSHIRE SAUCE

1 TABLESPOON FRESH LEMON JUICE

1 ONION, CHOPPED

½ BROWN SUGAR

2 DASHES HOT PEPPER SAUCE

2/3 CUP WATER

Place sausage in a large saucepan. Add water to cover and simmer over low heat for 1 hour.

Drain.

Remove sausage and set aside.

Preheat oven to 350 degrees F (175 degrees C).

In the same saucepan combine the Worcestershire sauce, lemon juice, onion, sugar, hot pepper sauce and water. Bring all to a boil, stirring. Place reserved sausage in a 9x13-inch baking dish and cover it with the sauce mixture.

Bake at 350 degrees F (175 degrees C) for 1 hour.

Entree

Baked Chicken Reuben

INGREDIENTS

6 SKINLESS, BONELESS CHICKEN BREAST HALVES
1/4 TEASPOON SALT
1/8 TEASPOON GROUND BLACK PEPPER
1 (16 OUNCE) CAN SAUERKRAUT, DRAINED AND PRESSED
4 SLICES SWISS CHEESE
1 1/4 CUPS THOUSAND ISLAND SALAD DRESSING
1 TABLESPOON CHOPPED FRESH PARSLEY

NOTE THAT IF SAUERKRAUT IS NOT AVAILABLE IN YOUR CITY (AS WAS MY CASE), YOU CAN USE SHREDDED CABBAGE. IF YOU WANT TO MAKE IT TASTE LIKE SAUERKRAUT, YOU CAN FRY THE CABBAGE WITH A LITTLE SALT AND VINEGAR TO SOFTEN IT.

Preheat oven to 325 degrees F (165 degrees C).

Place chicken in a lightly greased 9x13 inch baking dish. Sprinkle with salt and pepper. Place sauerkraut over chicken and top with cheese slices. Pour dressing over all and cover dish with aluminum foil.

Bake in preheated oven for 90 minutes, or until chicken is cooked through (fork can be easily inserted and juices run clear). Sprinkle with chopped parsley and serve.

Dessert

Chocolate Babka

INGREDIENTS

2 CUPS ALL-PURPOSE FLOUR
1/3 CUP UNSWEETENED COCOA POWDER
1 1/2 TEASPOONS BAKING POWDER
3/4 TEASPOON BAKING SODA
1 TEASPOON GROUND CINNAMON
1/2 TEASPOON SALT
1 CUP UNSALTED BUTTER
1 1/4 CUPS WHITE SUGAR
1 TEASPOON VANILLA EXTRACT
3 EGGS
1 CUP SOUR CREAM
1 CUP SEMISWEET CHOCOLATE CHIPS
1 CUP CHOPPED PECANS
1/4 CUP WHITE SUGAR
1 TEASPOON GROUND CINNAMON

Preheat oven to 350 degrees F (175 degrees C). Butter a 10-inch tube pan. Sift together the flour, cocoa, baking powder, baking soda, 1 teaspoon cinnamon, and salt; set aside.

In a medium bowl, beat the butter and 1 1/4 cup sugar with an electric mixer on high speed until light and fluffy. Change the mixer speed to medium, and beat in the vanilla. Beat in the eggs, one at a time. With the mixer on low speed, alternately beat the flour mixture and sour cream into the creamed mixture, beginning and ending with the flour mixture. Beat only until just blended.

For the topping:

In a small bowl combine the chocolate, pecans, 1/4 cup sugar, and 1 teaspoon cinnamon to make a crumb mixture. Spread half of the batter in the bottom of the prepared pan. Sprinkle with half of the crumb mixture. Pour in the remaining batter, and sprinkle with the remaining crumb mixture; press the crumbs in lightly so they adhere to the batter.

Quickly, but gently cut through the batter and crumbs in an up and down motion with a knife. Lightly tap the pan against a hard surface, to settle the batter.

Bake in the preheated oven for 40 minutes. Cover the top of the cake with aluminum foil. Continue baking until a skewer inserted halfway between the side of the pan and the tube comes out clean, about 20 minutes longer. Cool the cake in the pan on a wire rack for 30 minutes. Carefully loosen the cake from the sides of the pan. Invert cake onto rack, and cool completely.

Russia

Dedra's Notes

I was a Political Science major in undergraduate school, and I must say that Russia always fascinated me. It's not only the biggest country in the world, it's in the center of the action, bordering Europe and Asia, as well as two oceans. The terrain ranges from arctic forests to tropical beaches. Historical sites are rich with tales of valor and a great strength in the people to withstand any and all challenge. The cuisine is hearty and satisfying, and relatively low cost to prepare. More importantly, it's absolutely delicious!

Menu

Starter

Russian Mushroom and Potato Soup

Entree

Beef Stroganoff

– or –

Chicken Kiev

Dessert

Russian Tea Cakes

Starter

Russian Mushroom and Potato Soup

INGREDIENTS

5 TABLESPOONS BUTTER, DIVIDED
2 LEEKS, CHOPPED
3 MEDIUM CARROTS, SLICED
6 CUPS CHICKEN BROTH
2 TEASPOONS DRIED DILL WEED
2 TEASPOONS SALT
1/8 TEASPOON GROUND BLACK PEPPER
1 BAY LEAF
2 POUNDS OF POTATO, PEELED AND DICED
1 POUND FRESH MUSHROOMS, SLICED
1 CUP HALF-AND-HALF
¼ CUP ALL-PURPOSE FLOUR
FRESH DILL WEED, FOR GARNISH (OPTIONAL)

Melt 3 tablespoons butter in a large saucepan over medium heat. Mix in leeks and carrots, and cook 5 minutes. Pour in broth. Season with dill, salt, pepper, and bay leaf. Mix in potatoes, cover, and cook 20 minutes, or until potatoes are tender but firm. Remove and discard the bay leaf.

Melt the remaining butter in a skillet over medium heat, and sauté the mushrooms 5 minutes, until lightly browned. Stir into the soup.

In a small bowl, mix the half-and-half and flour until smooth. Stir into the soup to thicken. Garnish each bowl of soup with fresh dill to serve.

Entree

Beef Stroganoff

INGREDIENTS

2 ½ POUNDS OF BEEF CHUCK ROAST

½ TEASPOON SALT

½ TEASPOON GROUND BLACK PEPPER

4 OUNCES OF BUTTER

4 GREEN ONIONS, SLICED (WHITE PARTS ONLY)

4 TABLESPOONS ALL-PURPOSE FLOUR

1 (10.5 OUNCE) CAN CONDENSED BEEF BROTH

1 TEASPOON PREPARED MUSTARD

1 (6 OUNCE) CAN SLICED MUSHROOMS, DRAINED

1/3 CUP SOUR CREAM

1/3 CUP WHITE GRAPE JUICE

SALT TO TASTE

GROUND BLACK PEPPER TO TASTE

Remove any fat and gristle from the roast and cut into strips ½ inch thick by 1 inch long. Season with ½ teaspoon of both salt and pepper.

In a large skillet over medium heat, melt the butter and brown the beef strips quickly, then push the beef strips off to one side. Add the onions and cook slowly for 3 to 5 minutes, then push to the side with the beef strips.

Stir the flour into the juices on the empty side of the pan. Pour in beef broth and bring to a boil, stirring constantly. Lower the heat and stir in mustard. Cover and simmer for 1 hour or until the meat is tender.

Five minutes before serving, stir in the mushrooms, sour cream, and grape juice. Heat briefly then salt and pepper to taste.

Entree

Chicken Kiev

INGREDIENTS

1/3 CUP BUTTER
1/2 TEASPOON GROUND BLACK PEPPER
1 TEASPOON GARLIC POWDER
2 ½ POUNDS SKINLESS, BONELESS CHICKEN BREAST HALVES
2 EGGS
3 TABLESPOONS WATER
1/4 TEASPOON GROUND BLACK PEPPER
1/2 TEASPOON GARLIC POWDER
1 TEASPOON DRIED DILL WEED
3/4 CUP ALL-PURPOSE FLOUR
3/4 CUP DRY BREAD CRUMBS
2 CUPS VEGETABLE OIL FOR FRYING
1/2 LEMON, SLICED
1/4 CUP CHOPPED FRESH PARSLEY

Combine 1/3 cup butter, 1/2 teaspoon pepper and 1 teaspoon garlic powder. On a 6x6 inch piece of aluminum foil, spread mixture to about 2x3 inches. Place this mixture in the coldest section of your freezer and freeze until firm. This can be done ahead of time.

Remove all fat from the chicken breast. If using whole chicken breasts, cut them in half. Place each chicken breast half between 2 pieces of waxed paper and using a mallet, pound carefully to about 1/4-inch thickness or less.

When butter mixture is firm, remove from freezer and cut into 6 equal pieces. Place one piece of butter on each chicken breast. Fold in edges of chicken and then roll to encase the butter completely. Secure the chicken roll with small skewers or toothpicks.

In a mixing bowl, beat eggs with water until fluffy. In a separate bowl, mix together 1/4 teaspoon black pepper, 1/2 teaspoon garlic powder, dill weed and flour. Coat the chicken well with the seasoned flour. Dip the floured chicken in the egg mixture and then roll in the bread crumbs. Place coated chicken on a shallow tray and chill in refrigerator for 30 minutes.

In a medium size deep frying pan, heat vegetable oil to medium-high. Fry chicken for about 5 minutes then turn over and fry for 5 minutes longer or until the chicken is golden brown. To test for doneness, cut into one of the rolled chicken breasts to make sure it doesn't have a pink interior. Serve immediately, garnished with a sliced lemon twist and a sprinkling or parsley. This one turns out so good! Not the best choice if watching your waistline, however.

Dessert

Russian Tea Cakes

INGREDIENTS

1 CUP UNSALTED BUTTER, ROOM TEMPERATURE

1/3 CUP PACKED CONFECTIONERS' SUGAR

1 CUP FINELY CHOPPED TOASTED WALNUTS

1/8 TEASPOON SALT

1 1/2 TEASPOON VANILLA EXTRACT

2 CUPS ALL-PURPOSE FLOUR

2 TABLESPOONS ALL-PURPOSE FLOUR

1 CUP CONFECTIONERS' SUGAR FOR DUSTING, OR MORE AS NEEDED

Preheat oven to 350 degrees F (175 degrees C). Arrange rack in center position of oven.

Place butter, 1/3 cup packed powdered sugar, walnuts, salt, and vanilla in a bowl. Top with the flour. Mix with your clean hands until the dough starts to clump up. Keep mixing by hand until all the flour and clumps of butter are evenly mixed into the dough and it can be easily formed into balls.

Scoop out dough and roll by hand into uniformly round balls, just slightly larger than 1 inch. Place on a rimmed baking sheet lined with a silicone baking mat about 2 inches apart.

Bake in preheated oven until lightly golden, 15 to 25 minutes depending on the size of the cookies.

Let cool exactly 5 minutes then roll in a shallow bowl full of confectioners' sugar. Let cookies cool completely and toss them again in the confectioners' sugar. These cookies can be used for any occasion!

SPAIN

Dedra's Notes

Growing up in a small town in Alabama, I always dreamt of going to Spain and learning Spanish. When I got to the University of Alabama, I took two Spanish language courses, and I was getting pretty good at it, but sadly had no one to help me carry on with learning the language, so I forgot quite a bit. But I tell you one thing, I've never lost the desire to visit one day, and I've never stopped loving the food from there. The Land of Passion is a great name for this country, and the cuisine is an example of this passion.

Menu

Starter

Fried Empanadas

Entree

Alicante Style Chicken
– or –
Chickpeas and Chorizo

Dessert

Tarta De Queso

Starter

Fried Empanadas

INGREDIENTS

4 ½ CUPS ALL-PURPOSE FLOUR
1 ½ TEASPOONS SALT
½ CUP SHORTENING
1 ½ CUPS OF WATER OR AS NEEDED
2 TABLESPOONS OLIVE OIL
1 SMALL ONION, CHOPPED
1 ½ POUNDS GROUND BEEF
1 PINCH SALT
2 TABLESPOONS PAPRIKA
1 TABLESPOON CUMIN
½ TEASPOON GROUND BLACK PEPPER
¼ CUP RAISINS
1 TABLESPOON WHITE VINEGAR
2 HARD-COOKED EGGS, PEELED AND CHOPPED
1-QUART OIL FOR FRYING OR AS NEEDED

In a medium bowl, stir together the flour and salt. Cut in shortening using a pastry blender, or pinching into small pieces using your fingers, until the mixture resembles coarse crumbs.

Use a fork to stir in water a few tablespoons at a time, until the mixture forms a ball. Pat into a ball, and flatten slightly. Wrap in plastic wrap and refrigerate for 1 hour.

Heat the oil in a large skillet over medium heat. Add the onion and cook until tender. Crumble in the beef, and season with salt, paprika, cumin and black pepper. Cook, stirring frequently, until beef is browned. Drain excess grease, and stir in the raisins and vinegar. Refrigerate until chilled, then stir in the hard-cooked eggs.

Form the dough into 2 inch balls. On a floured surface, roll each ball out into a thin circle. Spoon some of the meat mixture onto the center, then fold into half-moon shapes. Seal edges by pressing with your fingers.

Heat oil in a deep-fryer to 365 degrees F (180 degrees C). Place one or two pies into the fryer at a time. Cook for about 5 minutes, turning once to brown on both sides. Drain on paper towels, and serve hot.

Entree

Alicante Style Chicken

INGREDIENTS

1 WHOLE CHICKEN, SKIN ON

ONE HEAD OF GARLIC, PEELED

A HANDFUL OF PARSLEY

1 TEASPOON SALT

2 TEASPOON BLACK PEPPER

1 CUP OF WHITE GRAPE JUICE

1 CUP OF WATER

EXTRA VIRGIN OLIVE OIL

1 CHICKEN OR VEGETABLE BOUILLON CUBE (OPTIONAL)

Preheat oven and a roasting pan to 400°F (200°C)

First, make sure that the chicken is completely dry, pat any moisture off with paper towels.

Put the chicken into a deep roasting pan.

In a food processor, or with a mortar and pestle, make a paste with the garlic cloves, salt, parsley and pepper. You can put the leftover paste in the fridge for later use.

Stuff the chicken with a couple of tablespoons of the paste, and cover it with a bit more. Then rub the skin with olive oil.

Pour the grape juice and water around the chicken, you can also add a chicken or vegetable bouillon cube if you want.

Cover the chicken in a damp piece of parchment paper.

Cooking time may vary, so you'll have to keep basting the bird and checking on whether it's done about every 15 min.

During the last 15 minutes in the oven, remove the parchment paper and let the skin become crispy. If it isn't crisping up, use the broiler for a few minutes.

Serve with homemade French fries or roasted potatoes.

Entree

Chickpeas and Vegan Sausage

INGREDIENTS

½ POUND DRY GARBANZO BEANS
1 RED BELL PEPPER
1 GREEN BELL PEPPER
1 TABLESPOON CANOLA OIL
4 RED POTATOES, CUT INTO ½ INCH CUBES
9 OUNCES' VEGAN SAUSAGE, (IF YOU CAN'T FIND
VEGAN SAUSAGE, USE VEGAN HOT DOGS) CUT INTO
½ INCH CUBES
1 YELLOW ONION, CUT INTO LARGE CHUNKS
8 CLOVES GARLIC, OR MORE TO TASTE
1 TEASPOON PAPRIKA
½ TEASPOON SALT, OR MORE TO TASTE
¼ CUP CHERRY CIDER SYRUP (OR IF YOU CAN'T FIND
THAT, USE ONE TEASPOON OF CHOCOLATE EXTRACT
MIXED WITH A TABLESPOON ON INSTANT COFFEE)

Put garbanzo beans into a large container; add enough cool water to cover by several inches.

Soak beans 8 hours to overnight. Drain and rinse before using.

Set oven rack about 6 inches from the heat source and preheat the oven's broiler. Line a baking sheet with aluminum foil.

Halve both the red bell pepper and green bell pepper from top to bottom. Remove and discard the stem, seeds, and ribs. Arrange pepper halves with cut sides down onto the prepared baking sheet.

Roast peppers under the pre-heated broiler until their skins have blackened and blistered, 5 to 8 minutes; transfer to a bowl and tightly seal bowl with plastic wrap to steam the peppers as they cool until the skins are loosened, about 20 minutes. Remove and discard skins. Slice peppers.

Heat canola oil in a pot over medium heat. Cook and stir potatoes in hot oil until browned, about 10 minutes; add sausage and continue to cook and stir until sausage is hot, 3 to 5 minutes more.

Stir peppers, onion, garlic cloves, paprika, and salt into the potato mixture; cook, stirring infrequently, until the onion softens, about 10 minutes more.

Stir soaked garbanzo beans into the mixture. Pour sherry cider (or alternate mix) over everything.

Bring the mixture to a simmer, reduce heat to medium-low, place a cover on the pot, and cook at a simmer until the beans are tender, 10 to 15 minutes.

Dessert

Tarte De Queso

INGREDIENTS

225 GRAMS (A LITTLE UNDER 8 OUNCES) OF
RICOTTA CHEESE (OR SIMILAR)
2 EGGS
70 GRAMS (5 T) OF UNSALTED BUTTER (AT ROOM
TEMPERATURE)
1 CUP SUGAR
1 CUP FLOUR
2 CUPS WHOLE MILK
2 TEASPOONS LEMON ZEST
1 AND A 1/2 TEASPOON VANILLA EXTRACT
SMALL PINCH OF SALT

Preheat the oven to 350°F (180°C)

Cream the butter and sugar and whisk in the eggs and vanilla.

Beat well and add in the ricotta cheese and pinch of salt.

Finally, beat in the milk and then, little by little, the flour.

Stir in the lemon zest.

Pour the mixture into a 9x13 inch baking dish and bake for between 35 and 45 minutes.

The Spanish cheesecake is ready when slightly browned and a toothpick comes out clean.

Let the cheesecake cool for at least 15 minutes to set.

Thailand

Dedra's Notes

I have a good friend who goes to Thailand for all her medical care needs, and I think she would agree that Thailand is indeed the land of smiles. She loved her time there and posted the most amazing pictures! I've not had the pleasure of visiting, but I somehow know in my heart that I will one day. In the meantime, Thai cuisine remains one of my favorites.

Menu

Starter

Thai Fish Cakes

Entree

Garlic Pepper Shrimp
– or –
Thai Chicken Satay

Dessert

Mango with Sticky Rice

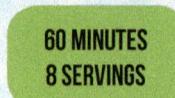

60 MINUTES
8 SERVINGS

Starter

Thai Fish Cakes

INGREDIENTS

1-POUND BONELESS FISH FILLETS, CUBED

½ CUP ALL-PURPOSE FLOUR

2 TABLESPOONS OYSTER SAUCE

2 TABLESPOONS SWEET CHILI SAUCE

1 TEASPOON FISH SAUCE

1 TEASPOON BROWN SUGAR

¼ CUP CHOPPED FRESH CILANTRO

4 GREEN ONIONS, SLICED

1 EGG

OIL FOR FRYING

Combine fish, 75g flour, oyster sauce, chili sauce, fish sauce, brown sugar, coriander, spring onions and egg in a food processor.

Process until well combined. Chill in the fridge for 30 minutes.

Shape mixture into fish cakes, and lightly dust with flour.

Pour oil into a heavy frying pan. Heat over medium-high heat until hot. Fry fish cakes for 8 -10 minutes, turning once, or until golden brown.

Entree

Spicy Garlic and Pepper Shrimp

INGREDIENTS

2 ½ TABLESPOONS VEGETABLE OIL

¼ CUP WATER

1 CUP SHREDDED CABBAGE

1 TABLESPOON MINCED GARLIC

8 LARGE FRESH SHRIMP, PEELED AND DEVEINED

2 TEASPOONS CRUSHED RED PEPPER FLAKES

2 TABLESPOONS SLICED ONION

1 TABLESPOON CHOPPED FRESH CILANTRO

1 TABLESPOON SOY SAUCE

Heat 1 tablespoon oil in a skillet over high heat. Add cabbage and 1 tablespoon water stir-fry for 30 seconds. Remove cabbage from skillet and place on a serving platter.

Heat the remaining 1 1/2 tablespoons oil in the skillet over high heat.

Place the garlic and shrimp in the skillet and stir until garlic is lightly browned and shrimp turns pink. Add pepper, onion, cilantro, soy sauce and remaining water to the skillet. Stir-fry for 10 seconds. Pour the hot mixture onto the cabbage.

Entree

Chicken Satay

INGREDIENTS

½ CUP CANNED COCONUT MILK
1 ½ TEASPOONS GROUND CORIANDER
1 TEASPOON YELLOW CURRY POWDER
1 TEASPOON FISH SAUCE
½ TEASPOON CHILI OIL
1 POUND SKINLESS, BONELESS CHICKEN BREAST
HALVES — CUT INTO STRIPS
1 TABLESPOON CHOPPED FRESH CILANTRO
1 TABLESPOON CHOPPED UNSALTED PEANUTS
13 WOODEN SKEWERS, SOAKED IN WATER FOR 15
MINUTES
1 CUP PREPARED THAI PEANUT SAUCE

In a medium bowl, stir together the coconut milk, ground coriander, curry powder, fish sauce, and chili oil. Add the chicken breast strips, and stir to coat. Cover, and refrigerate for at least 30 minutes, and up to 2 hours.

Preheat an indoor or outdoor grill for high heat. Thread the chicken strips onto skewers. Discard marinade.

Grill chicken for 2 to 3 minutes per side, until no longer pink. Time will depend on how thick your strips are. Transfer to a serving plate, and garnish with cilantro and peanuts. Serve with peanut sauce for dipping.

Dessert

Mango with Sticky Rice

INGREDIENTS

1 1/2 CUPS UNCOOKED SHORT-GRAIN WHITE RICE

2 CUPS WATER

1 1/2 CUPS COCONUT MILK

1 CUP WHITE SUGAR

1/2 TEASPOON SALT

1/2 CUP COCONUT MILK

1 TABLESPOON WHITE SUGAR

1/4 TEASPOON SALT

1 TABLESPOON TAPIOCA STARCH

3 MANGOS, PEELED AND SLICED

1 TABLESPOON TOASTED SESAME SEEDS

Combine the rice and water in a saucepan; bring to a boil; cover and reduce heat to low.

Simmer until water is absorbed, 15 to 20 minutes.

While the rice cooks, mix together 1 1/2 cups coconut milk, 1 cup sugar, and 1/2 teaspoon salt in a saucepan over medium heat; bring to a boil; remove from heat and set aside. Stir the cooked rice into the coconut milk mixture; cover. Allow to cool for 1 hour.

Make a sauce by mixing together 1/2 cup coconut milk, 1 tablespoon sugar, 1/4 teaspoon salt, and the tapioca starch in a saucepan; bring to a boil.

Place the sticky rice on a serving dish. Arrange the mangos on top of the rice. Pour the sauce over the mangos and rice. Sprinkle with sesame seeds.

Turkey

Dedra's Notes

The land of legends is very accurate! This is the land of what was once the most powerful empire on Earth. The Ottoman Empire has been a fascination of mine for a long time, and I have been to Turkey twice, I'm proud to say! There's so much to do here, but if you go, don't forget to visit the Topkapi Palace, as this was the home of almost every Sultan that the Empire knew, as well as the legendary Hurrem Sultan, the wife of Sultan Suleiman that shaped a nation. There's also a fabulous museum there where you can see a number of amazing artifacts of the Islamic world, including the Staff of Moses. But, while you're there, don't forget to eat from a wide variety of Kabab dishes as well as succulent spreads and freshly cooked Turkish bread! Don't be surprised if you have to let your pants out a little.

Menu

Starter

Red Lentil Soup

Entree

Chicken Kebab

– or –

Muhammara

Dessert

Turkish Delight

Starter

Red Lentil Soup

INGREDIENTS

1/4 CUP BUTTER

1 ½ ONIONS, FINELY CHOPPED

1 TEASPOON PAPRIKA

1 CUP RED LENTILS

1/2 CUP FINE BULGUR

2 TABLESPOONS TOMATO PASTE

8 CUPS VEGETABLE STOCK

1/8 TEASPOON CAYENNE PEPPER

1 TABLESPOON DRIED MINT LEAVES

4 SLICES LEMON

1/2 TEASPOON CHOPPED FRESH MINT

Melt the butter in a large saucepan over low heat. Cook the onions in the hot butter until they are golden brown, about 15 minutes.

Stir the paprika, lentils, and bulgur into the onions and coat with the butter.

Add the tomato paste, vegetable stock, and cayenne pepper; bring to a boil and cook until soft and creamy, about 1 hour.

Crumble the dried mint leaves into the soup; stir the soup and remove from heat.

Ladle into bowls and garnish with lemon slices and fresh mint to serve.

Entree

Turkish Chicken Kebab

INGREDIENTS

1 CUP WHOLE-MILK GREEK YOGURT
2 TABLESPOONS FRESHLY SQUEEZED LEMON JUICE, OR MORE TO TASTE
2 TABLESPOONS OLIVE OIL
2 TABLESPOONS KETCHUP
6 CLOVES GARLIC, MINCED
1 TABLESPOON ALEPPO RED PEPPER FLAKES
1 TABLESPOON KOSHER SALT
1 1/2 TEASPOONS GROUND CUMIN
1 TEASPOON FRESHLY GROUND BLACK PEPPER
1 TEASPOON PAPRIKA
1/8 TEASPOON GROUND CINNAMON
PINCH OF CAYENNE PEPPER
3 POUNDS BONELESS, SKINLESS CHICKEN THIGHS, HALVED
4 LONG METAL SKEWERS

Whisk yogurt, lemon juice, olive oil, ketchup, garlic, red pepper flakes, salt, cumin, black pepper, paprika, and cinnamon together in a bowl.

Place chicken thigh halves into the yogurt marinade and coat them thoroughly on all sides.

Cover bowl with plastic wrap and refrigerate 2 to 8 hours.

Preheat an outdoor grill for medium-high heat and lightly oil the grate.

Using 2 skewers for each kebab, thread half of the chicken thighs onto each pair of skewers making a fairly thick "log" shape.

Place kebabs on grill. Do not try to turn them until they begin to unstick from the grill, 3 or 4 minutes. Turn kebabs and grill the other side 3 or 4 minutes; turn.

Continue cooking and turning until chicken is no longer pink in the center and the juices run clear, about 6 minutes. An instant-read thermometer inserted into the center should read at least 165 degrees F (74 degrees C).

Entree

Muhammara

INGREDIENTS

4 TABLESPOONS OLIVE OIL, DIVIDED

1 1/4 CUPS RAW WALNUT HALVES

1 CUP FIRE-ROASTED RED BELL PEPPERS - PEELED, SEEDED, COARSELY CHOPPED

2 GARLIC CLOVES, CRUSHED

2 TABLESPOONS LEMON JUICE

2 TEASPOONS POMEGRANATE MOLASSES

1 TEASPOON SALT, PLUS MORE IF NEEDED

1 TEASPOON PAPRIKA

1 TEASPOON ALEPPO PEPPER FLAKES OR OTHER RED PEPPER FLAKES, PLUS A PINCH OR SO FOR GARNISH

1/2 TEASPOON CUMIN

1/2 TEASPOON CAYENNE PEPPER

1 TABLESPOON CHOPPED ITALIAN PARSLEY FOR GARNISH

Heat a skillet over medium heat. Add walnuts and drizzle with 1 tablespoon olive oil. Cook and stir frequently until walnuts smell toasted and are lightly browned, about 5 minutes. Remove from heat and transfer walnuts to a plate to cool. Reserve 2 or 3 to coarsely chop and use for garnish.

Place peppers in bowl of a food processor. Add walnuts, toasted bread crumbs, garlic, lemon juice, pomegranate molasses, salt, paprika, Aleppo pepper flakes, cumin, and cayenne pepper.

Drizzle with remaining 2 tablespoons olive oil.

Pulse on and off, scraping mixture down occasionally, until mixture is fairly fine and smooth.

Transfer to a bowl; cover and refrigerate until chilled, about 2 hours.

Transfer to a shallow serving bowl. Use the back of a spoon to swirl indentations on the surface to capture the garnishes. Garnish with reserved chopped walnuts, a drizzle of olive oil, pepper flakes, and chopped parsley. This dish can be a starter or a main course for Vegans, as it's quite satisfying with Vegan flatbread, prepared as sandwiches.

Dessert

Turkish Delights

INGREDIENTS

1 TEASPOON VEGETABLE OIL, OR TO TASTE

1 2/3 CUPS COLD WATER, DIVIDED

7 TEASPOONS UNFLAVORED GELATIN

2 1/3 CUPS WHITE SUGAR

3 TABLESPOONS STRAINED FRESH LEMON JUICE

4 TEASPOONS ROSE WATER

2 DROPS RED FOOD COLORING

1 TABLESPOON CORNSTARCH, OR AS NEEDED

Grease an 8-inch square pan with vegetable oil.

Place 2/3 cup water in a small bowl. Sprinkle gelatin on top; let stand until softened, about 15 minutes.

Combine remaining 1 cup water, sugar, and lemon juice in a saucepan over medium heat; bring to a boil, stirring until sugar dissolves. Increase heat and boil syrup, covered, for 3 minutes.

Uncover saucepan and attach a candy thermometer to the side; continue cooking syrup until the temperature reaches 238 degrees F (114 degrees C), about 5 minutes. Remove from heat; stir in gelatin mixture carefully until completely dissolved. Mix in rose water and red food coloring.

Pour syrup into the greased pan. Let stand at room temperature until gelled, about 4 hours.

Cover with plastic wrap and chill, 8 hours to overnight.

Cut gelled mixture into 1-inch squares. Dust with cornstarch.

U.A.E.

THE PEARL OF THE MIDDLE EAST

Oh how I love the UAE! I am very happy living here, and I absolutely love the food, but there's one thing that I must admit. UAE is a wonderful country, but since it's so small and so saturated with residents from more than 300 nationalities, almost all of the recipes are originally from somewhere else. The upside of this is that we are one of the most international nations in the world, with the best of everything, including food.

Menu

Starter

Samosas

Entree

Laham Machboos
– or –
Tofu Machboos

Dessert

Luqaimat

Starter

Samosas

INGREDIENTS

2 CUPS ALL-PURPOSE FLOUR
1/2 TEASPOON SALT
2 TABLESPOONS BUTTER
1/4 CUP WATER
1-QUART OIL FOR DEEP FRYING
2 TABLESPOONS BUTTER
1 SMALL ONION, CHOPPED
2 CLOVES GARLIC, CHOPPED
2 GREEN CHILE PEPPERS, CHOPPED
1 TABLESPOON FRESH GINGER ROOT, CHOPPED
1/2 TEASPOON GROUND TURMERIC
1/2 TEASPOON CHILI POWDER
3/4-POUND GROUND LAMB
1 TEASPOON SALT
2 TEASPOONS GRAHAM MASALA
1 1/2 TABLESPOONS FRESH LEMON JUICE

In a medium bowl, mix flour, salt and butter until the mixture resembles fine bread crumbs.

Pour in water, using more (up to approximately 1/4 cup) if necessary to make a smooth dough.

Pat into a ball. Place on a lightly floured surface and knead 10 minutes, or until dough is smooth and elastic. Return to the bowl, cover and set aside.

Heat oil in a large, deep skillet to 375 degrees F (190 degrees C).

Melt butter in a medium saucepan over medium high heat. Stir in onion, garlic, green Chile peppers and ginger. Cook 5 minutes, or until onions are golden brown. Stir in turmeric, chili powder, ground lamb and salt. Cook until the lamb meat is evenly brown, about 10 minutes.

Stir in graham masala and lemon juice. Continue cooking 5 minutes, then remove from heat.

Divide dough into 15 equal portions. Roll portions into balls, then flatten into 4 inch circles. Cut each circle in half. Dampen edges and form semicircles into cones. Fill cones with equal portions of the lamb meat mixture. Dampen top and bottom edges of cones, and pinch to seal.

Carefully lower cones into preheated oil a few at a time. Fry until golden brown, 2 to 3 minutes.

Drain on paper towels. Serve warm.

Entree

Laham Machboos

INGREDIENTS

5 LBS. GOAT MEAT

4 TABLESPOONS CANOLA OIL

3 MEDIUM ONIONS

2 TEASPOONS GARLIC PASTE

2 TEASPOONS GINGER PASTE

2 (14 1/2 OUNCE) CANS DICED TOMATOES

1/4 CUP YOGURT

1 TEASPOON CHILI POWDER

10 WHOLE CLOVES

8 GREEN CARDAMOM PODS

4 BLACK CARDAMOM PODS

10 BLACK PEPPERCORNS

1 TEASPOON CUMIN POWDER

2 TEASPOONS CORIANDER POWDER

2 TEASPOONS GRAHAM MASALA

2 TEASPOONS CURRY POWDER

1 CINNAMON STICK

4 TEASPOONS SALT

2 BAY LEAVES

10 DRIED PLUMS

4 FRESH GREEN CHILIES

2 TABLESPOONS FRESH CILANTRO

1 PINCH SAFFRON

9 CUPS BASMATI RICE

15 CUPS WATER

Soak rice for half an hour.

Cook in rice cooker with 15 cups of water. Cook rice until almost done.

Fry onions in oil until golden brown.

Add ginger and garlic.

Add chili powder, cloves, cardamom, pepper corn, cumin, curry, graham masala, coriander, cinnamon stick, bay leaves, dried plums, and salt.

Add yogurt.

Add tomatoes and cook until dry.

Add meat.

Add green chills.

Cook until meat is done and add water if needed.

Add cilantro.

Mix saffron with hot water.

Layer rice and meat mixture and sprinkle with saffron mixture.

Put in oven at 350°F for 20 minutes.

Entree

Tofu Machboos

INGREDIENTS

1 CUP BASMATI RICE
1 1/2 CUPS WATER
2 TABLESPOONS VEGETABLE OIL
1 MEDIUM ONION, MINCED
4 LARGE GARLIC CLOVES, FINELY MINCED
ONE 2-INCH PIECE OF GINGER, PEELED AND VERY FINELY MINCED
1/2 CUP DICED TOMATOES (FRESH, IF IN SEASON, OR CANNED)
4 GREEN CARDAMOM PODS
1/2 TEASPOON GROUND CORIANDER
1/2 TEASPOON GROUND CUMIN
1/4 TEASPOON CINNAMON
1 TEASPOON GRAHAM MASALA
1 TEASPOON SEA SALT
6 OUNCES OF MEDIUM FIRM TOFU, DICED
2 TABLESPOONS RAISINS
3 TABLESPOONS SLIVERED ALMONDS

Preheat the oven to 350°. In a small pot, combine the basmati rice and water and bring to a boil over high heat. Reduce the heat to the lowest setting, and cook, covered, for 15 minutes.

Remove from the heat and let it sit, covered, for 10 minutes.

In a large frying pan, heat the oil over medium high heat. Add the onion and cook until it is soft and light brown, about 7 to 8 minutes. Add the garlic and ginger and cook for 1 minute.

Add the tomatoes, cardamom pods, coriander, cumin, cinnamon, graham masala and sea salt and cook for 3 minutes. Remove from the heat and stir in the tofu, raisins and slivered almonds.

Put half of the rice in the bottom of an ovenproof dish. Next, layer in half of the tofu, the rest of the rice and finally the remaining tofu.

Cook, uncovered, in the preheated oven for 30 minutes.

Dessert

Luqaimat

INGREDIENTS

FLOUR NO. 1 — 500 GRAMS

CORN FLOUR — 200 GRAMS

BAKING POWDER — 100 GRAMS

YEAST — 2 TEASPOONS

SUGAR — 4 TEASPOONS

OIL

SAFFRON — A PINCH

CARDAMOM

DATE SYRUP

MILK — 100ML

Mix the flour, corn flour, baking powder and yeast.

Add sugar and crushed cardamom.

Heat the milk with oil and add saffron for color and flavor.

Mix everything together well and allow the dough to rise for half an hour.

Make tiny balls out of the dough and deep fry in oil at 160c.

When the dumplings are light brown, remove from oil and place it on kitchen paper.

Serve hot with date syrup.

UKRAINE

THE LAND OF WONDERS

I've never visited the Ukraine, but I absolutely love the fact that this country has the most wonders of the world. If you really take a close look, much of this nation looks like something you'd see out of the pages of a fairytale. Their cuisine is extremely similar to Russian, but I've collected a few here that are more exclusive to Ukraine.

Menu

Starter

Eggplants Mezhivo

Entree

Ukrainian Goulash

– or –

Chicken Paprikash

Dessert

Country Babka

Starter

Eggplant Mezhivo

INGREDIENTS

EGGPLANT 500 G

TOMATOES 200 G

ONIONS 200 G

VEGETABLE OIL 2 TBSP.

TABLE VINEGAR 1 TBSP.

SUGAR 1 TBSP.

GROUND BLACK PEPPER TO TASTE

SHREDDED PARSLEY 50 G

Wash the eggplants. Trim off the stem end, cut them widthwise, and season both sides with salt and pepper.

Fry the eggplant slices until they have a golden crisp. Put them into the casserole.

Chop and then brown the onion in the frying pan. Add the browned onion to the eggplants.

Wash and chop the tomatoes; slightly fry them over low heat in a little of vegetable oil. Rub the tomatoes through the sieve to obtain the tomato paste.

Combine the tomato paste with vinegar, sugar, salt and pepper. Stir the mix well. Pour it off to the eggplants, and braise over low heat for 12-15 mins.

The eggplant mezhivo should be served cooled, previously dressed with shredded parsley.

Entree

Ukrainian Goulash

INGREDIENTS

2 TABLESPOONS VEGETABLE SHORTENING
2 POUNDS CUBED BEEF STEW MEAT
2 ONIONS, SLICED
1 CLOVE GARLIC, MINCED
1 TABLESPOON PAPRIKA
1 1/2 TEASPOONS SALT
1/8 TEASPOON GROUND BLACK PEPPER
2 CUPS WATER
1 CUP STEAK SAUCE
1 TABLESPOON ALL-PURPOSE FLOUR
2 TABLESPOONS WATER

Melt shortening in a large pot over medium heat. Cook beef in hot shortening until completely browned, 5 to 7 minutes. Stir onion, garlic, paprika, salt, and pepper into the beef; cook and stir 5 minutes more.

Pour water and steak sauce into the pot; stir until beef mixture is evenly coated. Bring the mixture to a simmer, reduce heat to low, and cook until the beef is tender, about 15 minutes.

Whisk flour into the water in a small bowl; stir into the beef mixture. Continue simmering stew until slightly thickened, 2 to 3 minutes.

Entree

Chicken Paprikash

INGREDIENTS

6 CHICKEN-BREAST HALVES, SKINLESS AND BONELESS
6 LARGE ONIONS, SLICED
6 CLOVES GARLIC, MINCED
1/2 CUP BUTTER
3 TBS. SWEET PAPRIKA POWDER
1 CUP RED GRAPE JUICE
1 CUP SOUR CREAM
1 TSP. GRANULAR SUGAR
SALT AND PEPPER TO TASTE

Lightly pound the chicken breasts with a meat mallet, to slightly flatten it, and break up the fibers.

In a large skillet, sauté onions in 1/2 cup of butter, until transparent.

Add garlic and paprika.

Sauté another minute.

Stir in the salt, pepper, and the red grape juice.

Push the onions to the side of the pan, and place the chicken breasts in the pan.

Cover chicken with sautéed onions, and cook about 10 minutes on one side.

Roll off the onions, turn over the chicken, cover with onions again, and cook for another 10 minutes.

Remove the chicken from the pan, and arrange it in a serving platter, cover, and set aside.

Add the sour cream into the onion mixture, and stir until fully incorporated. Mix in the sugar.

Pour the onion sauce over the chicken.

Serve hot, with pasta, or rice.

Dessert

Country Babka

INGREDIENTS

2 TEASPOONS WHITE SUGAR
1/2 CUP LUKEWARM WATER
2 (.25 OUNCE) PACKAGES ACTIVE DRY YEAST
1 CUP MILK, SCALDED AND COOLED
1 CUP ALL-PURPOSE FLOUR
6 EGGS
1 TEASPOON SALT
1 CUP WHITE SUGAR
1 CUP BUTTER, MELTED
2 TABLESPOONS LEMON ZEST
5 1/2 CUPS BREAD FLOUR
1 CUP RAISINS

In a small bowl, combine 2 teaspoons sugar, 1/2 cup water, yeast, milk and 1 cup flour. Mix until well blended, then cover and allow to rise in a warm place until light and bubbly, about 30 minutes.

In a large bowl, beat the eggs, salt and 1 cup white sugar until light and fluffy. Stir in the melted butter and lemon zest. Stir in the sponge, then gradually mix in the flour. Knead in the bowl for about 10 minutes, then knead in the raisins. Cover and let rise in a warm place until doubled in volume.

Punch down dough and knead for a couple of turns then let it rise again. Grease 4 smaller coffee cans with soft butter. Fill the prepared pans about 1/3 full and let rise until the dough is even with the rim. Preheat the oven to 400 degrees F (200 degrees C).

Bake for 15 minutes in the preheated oven, then turn down the temperature to 350 degrees F (175 degrees C). Continue baking the bread for another 40 minutes. Avoid letting the top get too brown, if it begins to brown too quickly, cover the top with aluminum foil. Remove baked loaves from the pans and cool on a wire rack.

U.S.A.

Dedra's Notes

The last country featured is the first for me, as it's the place I grew up, and where I got my core values and ideas. America is truly special in the world—beautiful and vast, with so many cultures all blended into one place! It's so important to remember that this is what makes America great, the fact that the strength of many people have been joined together to form one Union. When it comes to cuisine, Americans have a unique ability to come up with original dishes that's all their own, but with a hint of the ancient past. I've chosen to present the Southern cuisine because that's what I know the most about, and since us Southerners are the King of Desserts, I've included a Pecan Pie. Enjoy!

Menu

Starter

Spinach and Strawberry Salad

Entree

Southern Fried Chicken

– or –

Macaroni and Cheese

Dessert

Pecan Pie

Starter

Spinach and Strawberry Salad

INGREDIENTS

2 BUNCHES SPINACH, RINSED AND TORN INTO
BITE-SIZE PIECES
4 CUPS SLICED STRAWBERRIES
1/2 CUP VEGETABLE OIL
1/4 CUP WHITE WINE VINEGAR
1/2 CUP WHITE SUGAR
1/4 TEASPOON PAPRIKA
2 TABLESPOONS SESAME SEEDS
1 TABLESPOON POPPY SEEDS

In a large bowl, toss together the spinach and strawberries.

In a medium bowl, whisk together the oil, vinegar, sugar, paprika, sesame seeds, and poppy seeds. Pour over the spinach and strawberries, and toss to coat.

VEGAN FOOD

Entree

Southern Fried Chicken

INGREDIENTS

3 CUPS ALL-PURPOSE FLOUR
1 1/2 TABLESPOONS GARLIC SALT
1 TABLESPOON GROUND BLACK PEPPER
1 TABLESPOON PAPRIKA
1/2 TEASPOON POULTRY SEASONING
1 1/3 CUPS ALL-PURPOSE FLOUR
1 TEASPOON SALT
1/4 TEASPOON GROUND BLACK PEPPER
2 EGG YOLKS, BEATEN
1 1/2 CUPS NONALCOHOLIC BEER OR WATER
1-QUART VEGETABLE OIL FOR FRYING
1 (3 POUND) WHOLE CHICKEN, CUT INTO PIECES
1 TEASPOON OF HOT SAUCE

In one medium bowl, mix together 3 cups of flour, garlic salt, 1 tablespoon black pepper, paprika and poultry seasoning. In a separate bowl, stir together 1 1/3 cups flour, salt, 1/4 teaspoon pepper, egg yolks and nonalcoholic beer. You may need to thin with additional beer if the batter is too thick.

Heat the oil in a deep-fryer to 350 degrees F (175 degrees C). Moisten each piece of chicken with a little water, then dip in the dry mix. Shake off excess and dip in the wet mix, then dip in the dry mix once more.

Carefully place the chicken pieces in the hot oil. Fry for 15 to 18 minutes, or until well browned. Smaller pieces will not take as long. Large pieces may take longer. Remove and drain on paper towels before serving. Remember that brown meat takes longer to fry than the white meat.

Entree

Real American Macaroni and Cheese

INGREDIENTS

1 (16 OUNCE) PACKAGE ELBOW MACARONI

1/4 CUP BUTTER

1/4 CUP ALL-PURPOSE FLOUR

1/4 TEASPOON DRIED THYME

1/4 TEASPOON CAYENNE PEPPER

1/8 TEASPOON WHITE PEPPER

3 CUPS MILK

1 PINCH GROUND NUTMEG

1/4 TEASPOON WORCESTERSHIRE SAUCE

1 TEASPOON SALT

3 CUPS SHREDDED SHARP CHEDDAR CHEESE, DIVIDED

1 TEASPOON DIJON MUSTARD

1/2 CUP PANKO BREAD CRUMBS

1 TABLESPOON BUTTER, MELTED

Preheat oven to 400 degrees F (200 degrees C).

Fill a large pot with lightly salted water and bring to a rolling boil over high heat. Once the water is boiling, stir in the macaroni, and return to a boil. Cook the pasta uncovered, stirring occasionally, until the pasta is cooked through but still slightly firm, about 8 minutes. Drain well.

Melt 1/4 cup butter in a large saucepan over medium heat. When the butter starts to foam and bubble, stir in the flour; cook on medium heat until flour just begins to turn pale yellow, 3 to 4 minutes. Add thyme, cayenne pepper, and white pepper; cook and stir another minute, then whisk in 1 cup of milk until smooth. Pour in remaining milk and whisk again. Bring the sauce just to a simmer.

Stir in nutmeg, Worcestershire sauce, and salt; simmer on medium-low heat until thickened, about 8 minutes, whisking often. Turn heat off, then add 2 1/4 cups of Cheddar cheese; stir until melted and combined. Add Dijon mustard.

Transfer the macaroni into a casserole dish, then pour in the cheese sauce; stir to thoroughly combine sauce with pasta. Mix panko bread crumbs and 1 tablespoon melted butter in a small bowl, and sprinkle crumbs on top of macaroni and cheese. Sprinkle remaining 3/4 cup of

Cheddar cheese on top.

Bake in the preheated oven until bread crumbs and Cheddar cheese topping are golden brown, about 20 minutes.

MINUTES
10 SERVINGS

Dessert

Pecan Pie

INGREDIENTS

1 3/4 CUPS WHITE SUGAR
1/4 CUP DARK CORN SYRUP
1/4 CUP BUTTER
1 TABLESPOON COLD WATER
2 TEASPOONS CORNSTARCH
3 EGGS
1/4 TEASPOON SALT
1 TEASPOON VANILLA EXTRACT
1 1/4 CUPS CHOPPED PECANS
1 (9 INCH) UNBAKED PIE SHELL

Preheat oven to 350 degrees F (175 degrees C).

In a medium saucepan, combine the sugar, corn syrup, butter, water, and cornstarch. Bring to a full boil, and remove from heat.

In a large bowl, beat eggs until frothy. Gradually beat in cooked syrup mixture. Stir in salt, vanilla, and pecans. Pour into pie shell.

Bake in preheated oven for 45 to 50 minutes, or until filling is set.

Extra Bits and Pieces

I hope you've enjoyed this journey around the world, and that you find just as much joy preparing these beautiful dishes for your family as I did. I remember many wonderful Ramadan nights, enjoying the food and the good company, as it's a tradition to invite friends over for the breaking of the fast.

Since I know that you'll probably want some tasty side dishes to pair with some of the meals, and a few extra desserts and some breakfast ideas, I decided to tack on a few in this final chapter. Additionally, a few of my friends, who happen to be chefs or food enthusiasts, have shared one of their signature dishes with you as well.

I've carefully selected dishes that are easy, nutritious, tasty and beautiful. I think you'll find them useful for everyday cooking as well as holiday cooking. The instructions are very easy to follow, and the ingredients aren't hard to find, and as in the menu, I've tried to include a generous amount of vegan options as well. Enjoy!

The following are 5 side dish recipes that can be paired with a majority of the meal plans that I've laid out in the previous chapters. I usually put out one green side dish and one yellow or orange. These are all nutritious and incredibly easy to prepare.

Side Dish

10 MINUTES
5 SERVINGS

Garlic and Onion Kale

INGREDIENTS

1 BUNCH KALE

1 TABLESPOON OLIVE OIL

1 TEASPOON MINCED GARLIC

½ SMALL ONION THINLY SLICED

Soak kale leaves in a large bowl of water until all dirt and sand begin to fall to the bottom, about 2 minutes. Lift kale from the bowl without drying the leaves and immediately remove and discard stems. Chop the kale leaves into 1-inch pieces.

Heat olive oil in a large skillet over medium heat; cook and stir garlic and onion until sizzling, about 1 minute. Add kale to the skillet and place a cover over the top.

Cook, stirring occasionally with tongs, until kale is bright green and slightly tender, 5 to 7 minutes. By the way, Kale is a superfood, packed with nutrients, so eat this often!

Side Dish

INGREDIENTS

2 CUPS WATER

1 CUP PEARL (ISRAELI) COUSCOUS

1 TABLESPOON OLIVE OIL

1/2 CUP CHOPPED YELLOW ONION

1 SHALLOT, CHOPPED

6 CLOVES GARLIC, QUARTERED

1/2 CUP GOLDEN RAISINS

1/2 CUP CHOPPED OIL-PACKED SUN-DRIED

TOMATOES

1/2 CUP SLIVERED ALMONDS

1/2 TEASPOON SALT

1/4 TEASPOON GROUND BLACK PEPPER

3 TABLESPOONS LEMON JUICE

1 TABLESPOON VEGAN BUTTER (OR REGULAR

BUTTER IF YOU ARE NOT VEGAN), SOFTENED

Moroccan Couscous

Bring the water to a boil in a saucepan; stir couscous into the boiling water and cook until couscous absorbs all the water and is cooked through, 10 to 15 minutes.

Heat olive oil in a skillet over medium-low heat; cook and stir onion, shallot, and garlic in the hot oil until onion is lightly browned, 15 to 20 minutes. Stir raisins, sun-dried tomatoes, and almonds into onion mixture; cook and stir until heated through, about 5 minutes.

Stir couscous into onion-raisin mixture; cook and stir until heated through, about 5 minutes. Season couscous mixture with salt and pepper; add lemon juice. Remove skillet from heat and stir butter into couscous mixture.

Side Dish

Roasted Garlic Broccoli

INGREDIENTS

1-POUND BROCCOLI

1/4 CUP OLIVE OIL

1 TABLESPOON RICE VINEGAR

6 CLOVES GARLIC, PEELED

1 TEASPOON SALT

RED PEPPER FLAKES, OPTIONAL

LEMON WEDGES, TO GARNISH

VEGAN FOOD

Heat the oven to 450°F. Cut the broccoli into bite-sized florets, and slice the stems into diagonal bite-sized pieces.

Blend the olive oil, rice vinegar, garlic, and salt in a small food processor until thick and creamy, or you can crush the garlic in a mortar and whisk in a bowl with the other dressing ingredients. If desired, add a pinch of red pepper flakes. (I'd definitely do this.) Toss with the broccoli and spread on a baking sheet.

Roast for 12 to 15 minutes or until broccoli is tender and the edges are singed. If you desire an extra measure of smokiness, switch the oven to broil, and move the baking sheet up to the highest rack. Broil for 1 to 2 minutes.

Arrange nicely on a plate with pretty lemon slices on the side.

Side Dish

INGREDIENTS

6 SWEET POTATOES, CUT INTO FRENCH FRIES
2 TABLESPOONS CANOLA OIL
3 TABLESPOONS TACO SEASONING MIX
1/4 TEASPOON CAYENNE PEPPER

Baked Sweet Potato Fries

Preheat the oven to 425 degrees F (220 degrees C).

In a plastic bag, combine the sweet potatoes, canola oil, taco seasoning, and cayenne pepper.

Close and shake the bag until the fries are evenly coated. Spread the fries out in a single layer on two large baking sheets.

Bake for 30 minutes, or until crispy and brown on one side. Turn the fries over using a spatula, and cook for another 30 minutes, or until they are all crispy on the outside and tender inside.

Thinner fries may not take as long.

Side Dish

Simple Mashed Potatoes

INGREDIENTS

2 POUNDS BAKING POTATOES, PEELED AND QUARTERED
2 TABLESPOONS BUTTER
1 CUP MILK
SALT AND PEPPER TO TASTE

Bring a pot of salted water to a boil. Add potatoes and cook until tender but still firm, about 15 minutes; drain.

In a small saucepan heat butter and milk over low heat until butter is melted. Using a potato masher or electric beater, slowly blend milk mixture into potatoes until smooth and creamy.

Season with salt and pepper to taste. (It's simply amazing how many people use a boxed mix of mashed potatoes when you can have fresh cooked ones so easily.)

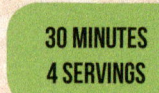

30 MINUTES
4 SERVINGS

International Breakfast

Even during Ramadan, when all the meals are served at night, occasionally, we missed breakfast food and decided to have a breakfast Iftar. The following are just a few international choices for breakfast, so instead of your usual quick and easy breakfast, why not opt for something more special?

INGREDIENTS

2 TBSP. OLIVE OIL
2 ONIONS, SLICED
1 RED OR GREEN PEPPER, HALVED DESEEDED AND SLICED
1-2 RED CHILI PEPPERS, DESEEDED AND SLICED
400G CAN CHOPPED TOMATOES
1-2 TSP CASTER SUGAR
4 EGGS
SMALL BUNCH PARSLEY, ROUGHLY CHOPPED
6 TBSP. THICK, CREAMY YOGURT
2 GARLIC CLOVES, CRUSHED

Menemen

Heat the oil in a heavy-based frying pan. Stir in the onions, pepper and chilies. Cook until they begin to soften. Add the tomatoes and sugar, mixing well. Cook until the liquid has reduced, season.

Using a wooden spoon, create 4 pockets in the tomato mixture and crack the eggs into them.

Cover the pan and cook the eggs over a low heat until just set.

Beat the yogurt with the garlic and season. Sprinkle the menemen with parsley and serve from the frying pan with a dollop of the garlic-flavored yogurt.

Sweet Breakfast Porridge

INGREDIENTS

1 CUP WHOLE MILK
4 CUPS WATER
4 CUPS WATER
1 TEASPOON SALT
1 CUP STONE-GROUND YELLOW CORNMEAL
1 TABLESPOON ALL-PURPOSE FLOUR
3 TABLESPOONS SWEETENED CONDENSED MILK
1 TEASPOON GROUND CINNAMON
1 TEASPOON VANILLA EXTRACT

In a large saucepan, combine the milk, water, and salt.

Whisk the cornmeal, and then the flour, into the cold liquid; then continue whisking while bringing to a boil over medium heat.

As soon as it comes to a boil, reduce the heat to maintain a light simmer. Whisk in the sweetened condensed milk, cinnamon, and vanilla.

Continue cooking, whisking frequently, until the porridge is soft and creamy, about 40 minutes. (The porridge will taste like porridge at this point and not cornmeal.) Serve immediately.

International Breakfast

Foul Medames

INGREDIENTS

1 CAN COOKED FAVA BEANS
1 MEDIUM TOMATO, FINELY CHOPPED
1 LEMON, JUICED
1/4 CUP MINT LEAVES CHOPPED
EXTRA VIRGIN OLIVE OIL TO DRIZZLE ON TOP
1 CLOVE GARLIC MINCED

In a small pan, heat the fava beans (including its canning water) on medium heat, till it boils.

Lower the heat and simmer for few minutes

Take off heat; mash with a pestle or the back of a spoon, but don't mash it all the way, like mashed potatoes. Leave lumps. Note that the picture depicts a non-mashed version of this dish.

You can also choose this way if you like.

Add the tomatoes and mint, reserving some for decoration

Pour mixture in a serving plate, top with remaining mint and tomatoes

Drizzle with olive oil.

International Breakfast

INGREDIENTS

2 CUPS WATER
1 1/4 CUPS MILK
1 TEASPOON SALT
1 CUP QUICK COOKING GRITS, NOT INSTANT (QUAKER IS A GOOD BRAND)
1/2 CUP BUTTER

Real Southern Grits

In a small pot, bring water, milk, and salt to a boil.

Slowly stir grits into boiling mixture. Stir continuously and thoroughly until grits are well mixed.

Let the pot return to a boil, cover pot with a lid, lower the temperature, and cook for approximately 30 minutes stirring occasionally. Add more water if necessary.

Grits are done when they have the consistency of smooth cream of wheat. Stir in half the butter and serve with remaining butter divided equally on top of each portion, or serve with fruit or with a savory meal. Fry up a couple of slices of Turkey bacon and scramble a couple eggs, and you have the perfect Southern breakfast!

International Breakfast

Spanish Omelet

INGREDIENTS

3 SMALL POTATOES
4 EGGS
1 ONION
SALT
OLIVE OIL
CHILI POWDER

Peel potatoes and cut them into small cubes.

Add salt to potatoes, then fry until lightly crunchy. Olive oil is best for frying.

At the last 5 mins of cooking add the onion to the potatoes. When tender, transfer potatoes and onion to paper towels to drain.

Beat the eggs. Be sure to add a pinch of salt and a pinch of chili pepper.

Lightly coat frying pan with olive oil. Add the eggs, potatoes and onions and cook over low heat, flipping omelet once to cook other side.

Cooking is a creative process, and this recipe lends itself to your creativity! Add spices, herbs, meats, veggies and cheese to your taste. I like this with parsley and a little chopped tomato.

Extra Desert

INGREDIENTS

1 EGG
½ TBSP. SEMOLINA
2 CUPS MILK POWDER
1 TSP. ALL-PURPOSE FLOUR
2 TSP. BAKING POWDER
1 TSP. COOKING OIL
MORE COOKING OIL (FOR DEEP FRYING)
SEEDS FROM 5 CARDAMOM PODS
2 CUPS SUGAR
A FEW DROPS ROSE WATER ESSENCE
2 CUPS WATER

Gulaab Jaamun

Since we included a dessert in each country's chapter, we already have a great number of amazing desserts, but I really wanted to include a few bonus desserts, especially from the areas that were not covered in the book, just because they're so awesome. Enjoy!

In a pot dissolve sugar in water on medium heat to make a syrup. Add the cardamom seeds and cook to a boil. Remove from heat and set aside.

Mix together the rest of the ingredients into a dough and make into small balls (makes about 32 balls) and deep fry until brown. Add to the syrup.

Extra Desert

Real New York Cheesecake with Blueberries

INGREDIENTS

6 OZ. DIGESTIVE BISCUITS, CRUSHED
5 OZ. UNSALTED BUTTER, MELTED
1 TBSP. CASTER SUGAR
3 TABLESPOONS CORN FLOUR
7 CUPS FULL-FAT CREAM CHEESE, AT ROOM
TEMPERATURE
2 LARGE EGGS
4 OZ. DOUBLE CREAM
1 VANILLA POD SEEDS OR ½ TEASPOON VANILLA
EXTRACT
ZEST OF 1 LEMON
2 ½ CUPS BLUEBERRIES
3 TABLESPOONS CASTER SUGAR

Grease and line a 24cm spring form cake tin and preheat the oven to 180°C/350°F/gas 4.

Prepare the base. Mix the biscuits and butter in a bowl, press into the base of the tin and cook for 10 minutes. Cool on a rack.

Turn the oven to 200°C/400°F/gas 6. Combine the sugar and corn flour in a bowl. Add the cream cheese and beat with an electric whisk until creamy. Add the eggs and beat well.

Gradually add the cream, beating until smooth, then beat in the vanilla and zest.

Tip the mixture into the tin, level the surface and sit on a baking sheet and place in the center of the oven. Bake for 40–45 minutes until the top is browned and the filling set around the edges. A piece of foil over the top will keep it from browning too much.

Let the cheesecake cool, then put in the fridge for 3 hours or overnight.

Put the blueberries in a pan, sprinkle over the sugar and add a splash of water. Put on a low-medium heat to simmer gently for 10 minutes. Cool and serve with the cheesecake. This is absolutely delicious!

Extra Desert

INGREDIENTS

1 CUP BUTTER, SOFTENED
1/2 CUP WHITE SUGAR
2 CUPS ALL-PURPOSE FLOUR
4 EGGS
1 1/2 CUPS WHITE SUGAR
1/4 CUP ALL-PURPOSE FLOUR
2 LEMONS, JUICED

Lemon Bars

Preheat oven to 350 degrees F (175 degrees C).

In a medium bowl, blend together softened butter, 2 cups flour and 1/2 cup sugar. Press into the bottom of an ungreased 9x13 inch pan.

Bake for 15 to 20 minutes in the preheated oven, or until firm and golden. In another bowl, whisk together the remaining 1 1/2 cups sugar and 1/4 cup flour. Whisk in the eggs and lemon juice. Pour over the baked crust.

Bake for an additional 20 minutes in the preheated oven. The bars will firm up as they cool. For a festive tray, make another pan using limes instead of lemons and adding a drop of green food coloring to give a very pale green. After both pans have cooled, cut into uniform 2 inch squares and arrange in a checkerboard fashion.

Guest Chef

We are very honored to include a few generous contributions from a few guest chefs and food enthusiasts from around the world. The following are a few introductions and a selection of signature dishes! Enjoy!

Richard Dockett, Baker and Author, England

Pickle and Cheese Roll

INGREDIENTS

FOR THE DOUGH:
500G STRONG WHITE FLOUR,
325ML WATER,
25ML OLIVE OIL
10G INSTANT YEAST
10G SALT
50G DRIED ONIONS.

FOR THE FILLING:
300G CHEESE OF YOUR CHOICE, GRATED,
PICKLE OR CHUTNEY TO TASTE,
OLIVE OIL TO GREASE THE PAN,

Combine all ingredients and make a dough as usual. It will be drier than usual as the onion absorbs water but this is OK.

Knead by hand for 10 minutes or on slow speed in a mixer with dough hook for 6 minutes.

Cover and allow to rise for an hour or until doubled in size.

Oil a large baking tray well. Turn out the dough and gently work it into the oiled tray, making an even layer.

Paint the chutney evenly over the dough and sprinkle the cheese on top.

Lift and stretch the long side of the dough gently and roll it up into a sausage shape, sealing the edge.

Cut into five-centimetre-thick slices, turn them ninety degrees and lay them on their sides in the tray.

Allow to rise for thirty minutes, while you preheat the oven to 230°C.

Bake for 18-20 minutes, turning once, if you have a thermometer, the internal temperature should be more than 95°C.

Allow to cool for five minutes then place on a wire rack to cool.

Can be eaten warm or cold, but be careful if heating in a microwave, the cheese gets very hot!!

I'm Richard Dee, as well as baking bread, I write Science Fiction and Steampunk adventures. I'm a retired Master Mariner and Ships Pilot, living in Devon, England.

You can find me at https://www.richarddeescifi.co.uk, where there are details of my books and my cooking adventures.

Guest Chef

20 MINUTES
2 SERVINGS

Magda Hajduk, Food Stylist and Recipe Developer, Dubai

Salmon with Spinach and Tomato

INGREDIENTS

450G ORGANIC SALMON
2 ORANGES (JUICE)
2 TEASPOONS OF GRATED FRESH GINGER
2 CUPS OF FRESH SPINACH
1/2 CUP OF SUN DRY TOMATOES
2 KNOBS OF BUTTER
2 COOKING SPOONS OF FULL FAT CREAM
1 TEASPOON OF FRESH THYME
1/3 CUP OF CHOPPED SPRING ONION
100G JASMINE RICE
HALF OF TEASPOON CHILI FLAKES
SALT
PEPPER

In oven proof pan put skin down salmon, pour juice from 2 oranges add thyme, chili flakes, salt, pepper and cook in preheated oven on 200 degrees for 10 min covered with cooking foil.

After 10-15 min uncover and add to the dish spinach, ginger, sun dry tomatoes butter, cream and cook additional 5 minutes.

Served with cooked jasmine rice mixed with spring onion and butter.

Magda is a food stylist and recipe developer based in Dubai. With more than ten years in the food industry she has been exposed to a variety of cuisines and cooking styles. Magda has combined her love of food with her love of beauty and design. Her styling is often seen in editorials and advertising campaigns. Her love of design is combined with a great eye for color and sense of style which you can see in every detail.

Guest Chef

Muhammad Junaid Qureshi, Sous Chef, Pearl Continental Hotel, Pakistan

Mumammed has years of experience as a Sous chef, but his specialty is sweets, as he's not been employed by a notorious sweet shop in Abu Dhabi to prepare his signature dishes every day.

Harissa Nipkiya

Please note...
Before the cake is made, two kinds of syrup need to be prepared. One without butter, and one with butter. The one without butter is prepared first.

Ingredients:
50 grams of sugar
50 grams of water
1 tablespoon of orange flavoring
1 teaspoon of lemon salt
200 grams of glucose

Instructions:
Put water in a saucepan and heat until warm.
Mix all ingredients except lemon salt and heat until boiling.
Add lemon salt and stir.
Turn off heat and keep this syrup in a cool place like the fridge for use later in the cake mixture.

Cake Mixture Step:
Ingredients:
Dry Items:
Semolina 3 cups
Sugar ¼ cup
Coconut powder ¼ cup
Milk powder ¼ cup
Baking powder 1 teaspoon
Liquid Items:
Cold Sugar syrup 50ml
Yoghurt 50 grams
Water 50 ml
Whole Pistachio 200 grams for garnish

Instructions:
Combine all dry ingredients in one bowl and stir.
Combine all wet ingredients in another bowl and stir.
Combine wet and dry ingredients in another large bowl and mix well with your clean hands.
After well mixed, leave to sit for a half hour.
After 15 min, preheat oven to 250 degrees.
When the half hour is done, press the mixture into a square baking tray and sprinkle with whole pistachios for garnish.
Bake for 15 min, check the dish, then bake for approximately 25 min more.
Remove from oven, and when cooled, cut diamond shape pieces.

In the meantime, ...
Prepare the syrup with butter while the dish cooks.

Ingredients:
Sugar ¼ cup
Water ¼ cup
Lemon juice 2 tablespoon
Orange juice 3 tablespoon
Orange blossom 1 tablespoon
Glucose 50 ml
Unsalted butter 50 gm
Lemon salt ¼ teaspoon

Instructions:
Put water in one sauce pan until warm.
Mix all other ingredients inside except the lemon salt.
After mixture boils, add lemon salt.
Remove from heat and sprinkle this mixture on the cake.
When cooled, enjoy!

Guest Chef

Sucheta Phule, Filmmaker and Amateur Chef, India/Dubai

Kheer: An Indian Delight

INGREDIENTS

LONG GRAIN BASMATI RICE SOAKED IN WATER: 1 CUP
FULL CREAM MILK: 1 LITER
SLICED ALMONDS: 1 TABLESPOON
SLICED PISTACHIOS: 1 TABLESPOON
SAFFRON: 10-12 STRANDS SOAKED IN WARM MILK
CARDAMOM: 5 PODS, PEELED AND SEEDS CRUSHED COARSELY
SUGAR: 1 CUP

Pour the milk in saucepan and bring to boil.

Now, add the soaked rice and saffron strands.

Keep stirring for 20-25 minutes on low flame till the rice is cooked and milk reduced to a beautiful creamy consistency (till milk is approximately reduced to half). Add sugar and coarsely crushed cardamom seeds.

Luscious rice kheer is ready to serve. Garnish with sliced pistachios and almonds.

For the corporate German language trainer turned filmmaker, Sucheta Phule, the gamut of storytelling just expanded when she travelled the world for her work. She makes films that are socially relevant and touch human hearts, telling stories of everyday triumphs of human spirit. Her first feature film, 'The Journey to Her Smile' won awards, critical accolades and great audience response at various film festivals across the globe incl. Cannes, USA, UK, Africa, India, Indonesia, etc.

Sucheta's earliest food memory is going on weekly shopping walks to local Mandi in Pune with her grandmother. Her food connoisseur father and the ever hospitable mother made the most memorable meals for all the gatherings of litterateurs, poets, filmmakers at her filmmaker/writer father's home. Today she remembers her father when her food trails lead her to tucked away places in the world to find the most delectable flavors. She finds the same joy in street food as in the Michelin star restaurant. The beautiful process of designing a menu to executing it is something she attributes to her mother. A purist at heart, she doesn't mind fusion occasionally to bring out the best on the platter. An eclectic mix of all this makes her a great conversationalist making the dinner table a place for soul food too. This food artist believes that art cannot be encapsulated in a single form.

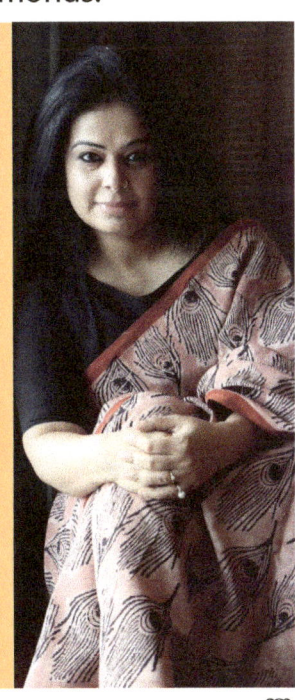

End Notes

I hope you've enjoyed this time with me, and I wish you all God's blessings and leave with you my hope for a brighter future, and more friendship and understanding among the cultures of the Earth. Please enjoy all these recipes with my heartfelt blessings, and please don't forget to join me on all social media channels to keep up with everything we do at Blue Jinni Media, as we'll surely be putting out more amazing projects soon!

Until next time, bon appetite and ...

Bye Now! Y'all Come Back Now, Ya Hear?

Dedra L. Stevenson, author, filmmaker, publisher, and all around foodie!

About the Author

Dedra L. Stevenson is the author of the acclaimed fantasy fiction trilogy, The Hakima's Tale, as well as the crime/courtroom drama, Desert Magnolia, and her first horror, The Skinwalker: Resurrection.

Dedra's also an award winning filmmaker, with a documentary called, Lemonade, which focuses on the needs of adults with Autism. Her next film, Just a Girl, is now in post-production, and is expected to be released by early 2019.

Links to all of her novels, podcasts and blogs can be found on www.bluejinnimedia.com and www.dedralstevenson.com.

In addition to her love for writing, she's got a passion for international cuisine, and is now ready to share what she's learned with you. The last chapter is called, "Bits and Pieces", and is a collection of a few more recipes that may be fun to use in everyday life—a few side dish options, breakfast options and a few contributions from guest chefs!

Enjoy this trip around the world!

Lightning Source UK Ltd.
Milton Keynes UK
UKHW050641081118
331819UK00005B/87/P

9 780464 992608